S0-DSO-393

IIE Research Report Number Twenty-two

daring to be different:

THE CHOICE OF NONCONVENTIONAL FIELDS OF STUDY BY INTERNATIONAL WOMEN STUDENTS

NELLY P. STROMQUIST,
University of Southern California

The Institute gratefully acknowledges
support from The Ford Foundation
for the research and publication of this report.

Contents

List of Tables

List of Figures

Acknowledgments

This study is the product of two concerns that had a happy convergence. For many years, I have been concerned with the existence of gender inequalities in society and with understanding the limits and potential of education in helping to improve the condition of women. Thus, I have had a long-standing interest in identifying ways to make the educational system serve the needs of women. I was fortunate to encounter Elinor Barber, then Director of Research at the Institute of International Education (IIE), who confronted me with two specific queries: why do so very few women study certain disciplines at the university level, and what are the processes that characterize the academic choices made by international women students? Working in an organization that coordinates study by international students in this country, she wanted information that could be used for some practical applications. Her concern for the policy implications of student decisions was a source of inspiration to me and prompted me to examine a field I had not considered before — that of higher education. Dr. Barber's insights, challenging questions, and persistent humor have been helpful at all stages of this study, and it is with gratitude that I acknowledge them.

I benefited from the comments to the study made by Drs. Eleanor Singer (Columbia University), Beatriz Schmukler (FLACSO, Argentina), Gerald Fry (University of Oregon), and Amaury Nora (University of Illinois, Chicago). At the University of Southern California, I was fortunate to have the research support of several capable and enthusiastic students: Patricia Poppe, EunSook Hong, and Betty Roy contributed in different ways to the realization of this study. These research assistants performed numerous tasks: some, like the application of soft-modeling techniques, demanded ingenuity; and others, like the monotonous tasks of mailing and coding questionnaires, required patience and alertness. I am particularly grateful to Patricia for her assistance in field testing the questionnaire during the summer of 1988 and for helping me classify the various fields according to their degree of conventionality. Eun-Sook was of great assistance in getting the software program for the LVPLS model to run smoothly in my microcomputer. Her assistance at times when my little machine refused to understand my awkward requests was invaluable. My thanks also to Sidi Abdullah, Shadidi Sia-Maat, Gaspard Bigumanshaka, and Raj Singh, doctoral students in the Division of Policy and Administration, who gave me hours of intense labor during various phases of the investigation.

I would like to express my gratitude to the directors and related personnel at the various international centers in the universities participating in this study: Ohio State University, the University of Minnesota, the University of Georgia, Stanford University, Columbia University, the University of California at Santa Cruz, Michigan State University, the University of Texas at Austin, the University of Wisconsin at Madison, and the University of Southern California. Without their generous assistance in allowing me access to international students in their respective universities, this study would not have been possible. I thank with deep gratitude the international graduate and undergraduate students who replied to the research questionnaire.

Last, but certainly not least, I wish to acknowledge the financial support of the Ford Foundation for the conduct of this study. I also wish to thank IIE, which, through the person of Dr. Barber, agreed to administer the grant and publish the results.

Introduction

Compared with their mothers, women today have a much greater chance not only of completing their baccalaureate but also of attaining an advanced degree. This progress in the participation of women in higher education has occurred in both developed and developing nations.

A further positive development in contemporary society is the increased access of women to new fields of study at the university level. This growth is of significant importance because it is anticipated that with new knowledge and skills, women will be able to attain positions and rewards based on their personal attributes rather than on ascribed characteristics. Higher education is of critical importance for women, because, even in an imperfect world, it facilitates access to positions of authority and leadership. Evidence from diverse cultural contexts indicates that education remains one of the most accessible means of social mobility: possessing a professional degree enables women to compete actively in the labor force and thus gain a significant measure of economic autonomy (for a recent synthesis of such findings, see Campbell and Laughlin, 1987).

To achieve positions of leadership and responsibility, women need not only to attain higher education, but to enter fields that have prestige in society and permit the introduction of new modes of thinking and new technologies. Therefore, it would seem that if social changes are shaped by people in key political and intellectual positions, the presence of women in those positions may contribute to policies that are sensitive to questions of gender equity and other forms of social justice. Women, unfortunately, still concentrate in what are known as "traditional" or "conventional" fields for women. Despite important inroads in the last decade, women are still underrepresented in managerial, scientific, and technological fields, all of them critical areas given the increasing role of science and technology in the rapidly changing work environment of the 21st century.

Due to various and mutually supportive mechanisms, women are guided and eventually choose themselves to move into fields that are sanctioned by society as being "proper" for their gender. What is considered an appropriate occupation only for women or only for men varies somewhat from country to country, but men's professional occupations are almost always more prestigious than those of women. When definitions of "gender appropriate" occupations persist for many years, certain occupations become designated as traditionally male or female, and the few women who venture into prestigious traditionally male disciplines are seen as going counter to social norms.

The clustering of women in a limited number of professions preempts the possibility of change in the definition of those fields because the dominant perspective of such fields, which is essentially a male perspective, will remain untouched. This perspective not only defines disciplines in narrow and often erroneous ways but also tends to attract into these fields minds that subscribe to those particular ways of understanding the world. In other words, male-defined disciplines produce the not surprising effect of appealing more to men than to women, thus reproducing the gender segregated nature of the disciplines.

The clustering of women in a few professions also eliminates women from positions of importance, in which they could be making decisions to alter the way technology and science is designed and applied. Having women in technological and scientific careers would not be simply a matter of better gender representation. It would be primarily a matter of giving women access to positions where decisions affecting critical social and economic outcomes originate. So the importance of women in scientific and technological positions is not cast merely in terms of prestigious positions, because to do so would be to endorse the arbitrary distinction of science as more valuable than other fields when in fact such a distinction has been used to "maintain existing class and gender relations in society" (Elliott and Powell, 1987). We have the expectation that the presence of women in science and technology will help redefine these fields by bringing to light perspectives and experiences heretofore ignored.

With the increased participation of the population in university studies, there has been a growth in the proportion of students from developing countries seeking education abroad. Data from a set of 13 countries indicate that the number of people who studied abroad in 1975 was 2.89 times that of 1969 and that in the short period of time between 1973 and 1975 it doubled. These statistics are surprising because they include several countries that are implementing special plans to develop their own higher education systems (Reiffers et al., 1982). The United States is a frequent choice for overseas study. The Institute of International Education (1989) reported a total of 366,350 international students in the United States for the 1988-89 academic year.

For individuals from developing countries who aspire to important positions in their fields, study abroad — particularly in the United States — is an effective investment. Study in U.S. universities is highly prestigious; hence, students who come to study here constitute a pool from which potential leaders will emerge. Although predictions of how many will become leaders are hazardous, one estimate holds that "one-third to one-half of the world's top positions in politics, business, education, and the military will be filled in the next 25 years by foreign students attending colleges and universities in the United States" (Lau, cited in Rentz, 1987, p. 10).

International students act as cultural carriers. They not only bring elements of their own cultural background to this country, but, more importantly, they also carry back to their countries of origin cultural elements from their hosts. Therefore, these students represent a vital human resource that must be fully prepared to undertake scientific and technical tasks as well as the more difficult challenges of improving their countries' social order.

If we are trying to promote changes in the conditions of women in society, particularly of women in developing countries — where often the degree of gender oppression is more evident and stronger — it becomes important to gain an understanding of how international students make their career choices and, especially, how female students select nonconventional fields of study, fields which are subject to considerable social gatekeeping. It would also be pertinent to understand whether the women who go into nonconventional fields have gender attitudes and professional aspirations that differentiate them from women in conventional fields of study, and, if so, how they differ. Finally, it would be useful to illuminate the university experience these graduate women undergo as they pursue nonconventional fields of study. If the university experience gives them further awareness of gender relations and significant professional involvement, then these students may go on to become committed, and socially aware professionals.

I.
The Logic of
Field Selection

Why do individuals select a given field of study? Why do most students choose to study fields that are very traditional for their gender while only few others adopt fields — and thus future occupations — that are considered highly nonconventional for their gender by most social standards?

There is a remarkable degree of stability in field selection by women and men. Despite the awareness and knowledge about gender disparities brought about by the feminist movement in the 70s and the subsequent creation of women's studies programs on numerous U.S. campuses, there is a strong tendency to maintain the current social definitions of what are appropriate disciplines and jobs for men and women. In a study of 100,000 high school seniors, Schoenmaker recently found that "the young men and women actually making an 'atypical choice' accounted for less than 5% of the total sample" (1988, p. 95). Schoenmaker, who defined as atypical those career choices which attracted less than 30 percent of individuals from a given sex, found that females making such atypical choices outperformed males in SAT scores by 100.31 points, particularly in math — a finding that suggests that women must be extremely competent to be able to enter nonconventional careers.

The selection of field by students will obviously determine the occupational positions these individuals will assume as they join the labor force. It is in the differential skilling and training by sex that a critical linkage takes places between the educational system and the labor market. As Connell states:

> Through such mechanisms the sexual division of labour is transformed into an apparently technical division of labour, resistant

to the more obvious antidiscrimination strategies. Where men are usually better prepared or trained than women for a given job, choosing "the best applicant" will normally mean choosing a man. (1987, p. 100)

Occupational choices by women have been the object of many studies in the last two decades. Variables thus far examined include: (1) background factors such as parental attitudes and occupations, role model influence, educational and academic success, particularly coursework in math and science, parental encouragement, and work experience; (2) personality factors such as self-efficacy and self-esteem; and (3) situational factors such as sex-appropriate occupational stereotypes, adult marital and parental status, and societal sex-role stereotypes (see Fassinger, 1985, for a detailed identification of the studies focusing on these variables). Most of these studies have examined isolated variables; one exception to this pattern is the study by Fassinger (1985), who proposed a causal model integrating various forces. Her model centered on the explanation of women's career choice, which was measured in terms of traditionality and prestige.

A number of theoretical explanations of occupational choices by women exist. Human capital theories trace differential occupational selection to differential training. These theories, based on the assumption of individual choice, assert that women, like men, seek education and training on the basis of a cost-benefit analysis of the costs of acquiring such skills and the benefits to be derived from them (in the form of higher wages or better consumption). These theories predict that a women's choice of disciplines and occupations will be different from men's since women want to maintain a crucial comparative advantage they have over men, namely bearing and raising children (Ram, 1982). Logical as this argument may be, it defines as a social advantage what other scholars — particularly feminist scholars — consider to be the very source of gender inequalities: the definition of women as essentially mothers. As Cole (1989) and others observe, human capital theories fail to explain why women tend to earn less than men with equal levels of education and why women are in such a limited range of occupations within skilled categories.

Other theories rely less on the individual's choice and assert that women end up in certain positions due to discrimination by employers in favor of men, which forces women into less prestigious and less well remunerated occupations (Becker, 1971; Ram, 1982). These theories place the burden for the emergence of job segregation on the employer and do not explain what forces lead employers to engage in such discrimination.

Feminist theories of occupational segregation offer a more complete and at times quite different logic. Some theorists claim that women constitute a reserve of labor, by which women are brought in as supplementary workers when the economy needs them and released when they are not needed (Hartsock, 1981).[1] This dynamic would lead to the employment of women in jobs with easy entry and exit, only in certain occupational categories. Other feminist theories concentrate on the explanation of male-female wage and prestige differences and trace these asymmetries to the existence of dual labor markets (a privileged primary sector and a disadvantaged secondary sector), in which women usually enter the secondary sector because it is to men's benefit to appropriate women's economic production (Delphy, 1977; Hartmann, 1979, 1981). Women's lower wages make women dependent on men within the family and enable men to keep women at home to provide services below market prices. These theories consider that the existence of occupational segregation in turn contributes to the development of gender-typed occupational preferences on the part of the individuals themselves. A related feminist interpretation postulates that an unwritten social contract reserves the best jobs for white men, and thus women — and other subordinated social groups — must choose from among a limited number of left-over, residual occupations, generally less prestigious and less well remunerated than those offered to white men (Strober, 1984).

Yet other theories for the differential occupations and educational choices that women make are based on socialization models, in which the inculcation of patriarchal values as the dominant ideology leads women to select jobs that are considered feminine or traditionally defined as proper for women (Douvan and Adelson, 1966; Clarricoates, 1980; Ashton and Maguire, 1980).

There are, then, a number of theories and empirical studies about occupational choices, but the literature on women's and men's choices of fields of study at the university level is sparse. However, two reasons justify focusing on field of study choices. First, academic fields are more precisely categorized than occupational choices. For instance, a person can have the occupational title of researcher, yet the research they do could be on teaching, biology, or nuclear engineering. A person can become an administrator, but he or she could be an administrator of nurses, of computer programmers, or of stock brokers. The second reason is that many individuals select fields of study without a full understanding of the specific occupation they will have upon graduation. In other words, the match between field of study and oc-

---

[1]There has been a criticism of the reserved labor force, because it should predict that women can replace all men's jobs (Cole, 1989), but, in my opinion, this is not necessary, because if there were total replacement, then there would be no social justification for defending gender asymmetries.

cupation, from the perspective of the individual's choice, is not always tight. Hence, field of study choices deserve to be understood in their own right.

The selection of fields by women is of special interest. Indeed, the question of whether self-selection occurs or whether individuals are channeled into a structurally determined range of choices has become part of an increasingly intense intellectual debate.

The literature identifies a number of factors behind academic field selection by individuals. These factors include: (1) the dynamics of the family environment, where parents provide continual role modeling and convey messages that shape students' choices; (2) the informal network of social actors for example friends, peers, and relatives; and (3) the school environment, an important setting for the socialization of individuals into academic choices, as the behavior and attitudes of teachers, counselors, and peers reproduce, and challenge gender-based modeling and messages (Clarricoates, 1980; Evans, 1982; Anyon, 1983; Gaskell, 1983).

Some research has focused on such factors affecting individual choices as the students' preparation and performance in the subjects needed to enter nonconventional fields for women (which call for mathematics, natural sciences, and related fields) and how well they think they did in those fields (Wiegers and Friezer, 1977; Schoenmaker, 1988). A smaller number of studies has focused on personality traits associated with certain professions. Natural scientists have been found to prefer "apartness from others: low interest in social activities, with neither preference for an active social life nor guilt concerning such tendencies toward social withdrawal" (Rossi, 1964, p. 622).

The literature is weak when it comes to the examination of field of study choices as a function of the individual's awareness of gender relations in society. For us, this is a fundamental question. If women who select nonconventional fields are also aware of the current functions of gender as a powerful social marker and of the need for women to take an active part in the transformation of social relations, then we would expect that these women will make a difference in the future of their societies. In the case of international female students, we would expect that if women in nonconventional fields have high levels of gender awareness they would be likely to contribute significantly to new forms of socioeconomic development in their respective countries and to the reconfiguration of social relations.

The purpose of this study is to find out why, in fact, international female students choose their fields and what values and attitudes are concomitant with these choices.

4

II.
A Gender-Based Inquiry Into Field Selection

In the examination of field selection from the perspective of gender as an ascribed social marker, choices are regarded with a certain degree of skepticism. To some degree, people autonomously develop predispositions that make them prefer one discipline to another. But it is clear that many of these dispositions are affected significantly by the social location of the individual and the symbols and representations that her or his social class defines as desirable for the members of that class (Bourdieu and Passeron, 1977).

Social representations and symbols derived from gender differences are numerous, widespread, and powerful. They orient individuals' psychological preferences. They create cultural obstacles. They produce material constraints and opportunities.

Depending on the strength of gender distinctions in a particular society, women face greater or lesser obstacles when they select nontraditional or nonconventional fields of study. Several factors increase the obstacles women may face; these include: the need to demonstrate greater competence than men in order to gain access to university programs leading to nontraditional careers; the need to make difficult choices between family and career lives; and the everyday discomfort attached to challenging subtle yet powerful and pervasive societal norms.

The socialization process women undergo encourages them to acquire nurturant and submissive traits. Some social scientists have asserted that women tend to be more caring and other-related than men (Gilligan, 1982; Neddings, 1984), and suggest that this socialization creates enduring personality orientations in women. This line of thought would imply the role of women's predispositions in the selection of conventional fields. An opposing view would see these orientations as more malleable and subject to change, given a proper alternative environment.

Theoretical Framework

This study sees field of study choices as the result of a confluence of factors deriving from individual and family characteristics as well as from more diffuse social representations of what are appropriate gender roles for family, work, and related social circumstances.

In the processes that affect the selection of a particular field of study, certainly the home environment looms significant. We consider this environment to be not only a source of gender ideologies but also a system of representations linked to material conditions. It is clear that the home environment reproduces gender relations and constitutes a central locus for the transmission of gender norms and identity (Delphy, 1977). What parents do on a daily basis, the occupational and family roles they fulfill, the expectations and aspirations they communicate to their children leave an imprint that has been well documented in socialization literature (Rosenberg, 1973). Children have been found to express well-defined, sex-typed occupational preferences, and such preferences seem already stable from ages 14 to 22 (Reskin and Hartmann, 1986). It is assumed that the greater the education of the parents and the greater the responsibility and prestige of their occupations and positions, the more parents will be able not only to offer a positive environment to their children but also to make an impact on them — parents in such positions are likely to function as powerful role models.

While the immediate family transmits through everyday practices the dominant logic regarding social relations, other social actors operate in the transmission of social definitions. On the matter of field of study selection, professionals in the schools are supposed — by the nature of the educational task they perform — to influence the career aspirations of students. Even though the contact of these actors is not as intense and long-lasting as that with one's immediate family, significant others in the form of teachers and counselors affect student choices of fields. These choices are formally predicated on basic individual competencies but, simultaneously, they are also affected by basic normative definitions of what constitutes femininity and masculinity in the immediate society. Individuals in the schools, including those in peer networks, make observations and provide advice regarding fields of study through one-to-one informal dialog or through more formal and distant forms of exposure. These contacts are not easy to document, but we can ask the individual to report who, according to his or her own recollection, played significant roles in field selection. We also assume that contacts with professionals in the prospective field also influence individual selections. The professionals in the field constitute concrete examples of people who went through a desired academic evolution; they also represent people whose work and family situations give a glimpse of what may happen to those selecting the same field of study.

In the case of women, the concept of accumulated disadvantage holds particular analytical promise. The concept is explained by Moore in this way:

> Some of the advantages men enjoy disproportionately include admission to the best graduate programs, receipt of better financial arrangements, selection as protégés of prominent and productive scholars, and introduction and participation in collegial networks where resources, advice, and insider information are dispersed (1987, p. 29).

While the concept of cumulative advantage would be better examined through longitudinal approaches or life history techniques, a crosssectional study can use this concept by looking at the interrelationship among social experiences and by reconstructing and connecting events at key transitional points in the life of the individual. In our case, these key points are construed to have occurred at the high school, undergraduate, and graduate levels.

A key concern in our study is the identification of the circumstances and factors that lead women to select nonconventional fields of study. This choice may be a form of defiance, because it goes counter to dominant definitions of what is appropriate for women. Often, individuals select a field because they associate it with social prestige. We hypothesize that individuals may be persuaded to select nonconventional fields if they associate these fields with high prestige. In other words, one of the reasons why individuals may be willing to go counter to traditional expectations in their fields of study might be that the level of prestige attached to that field outweighs the negative social costs associated with selecting fields not appropriate for their gender.

Additional important factors affecting individual choices are the students' own preparation in subjects needed to enter nonconventional fields for women (which call for competencies in subjects such as mathematics, natural sciences, and related fields) and how well they did in those fields.

We hypothesize further that if for some women the selection of nonconventional fields is a form a social defiance, then these women should evince a greater level of awareness than others regarding gender situations in their society. As women realize that there are gender inequalities in two of the most dominant social structures, the labor market and education, they will move into nonconventional studies as personal acts of defiance toward the established order. This notion is similar to that of "role transcenders," used by Angrist and Almquist (1975) to refer to persons who overcome the limits set by sex-role stereotyping. We would expect these women more strongly to endorse feminist attitudes than women in conventional fields. These women would be expected to have a strong set of attitudes that would call for the presence of women in multiple arenas and for the reduction of power differentials between the sexes.

It is important for the study to identify the relationship between the women's view of gender in society and their levels of feminism, on the one hand, and the selection of a nonconventional field of study, on the other, because a key assumption is frequently made that the increased presence of women in nonconventional fields of study will lead to societal changes. Presumably, these changes will happen not simply because the new professionals in key areas of social and economic life will be women but because these women will bring to these arenas more advanced understanding of gender and social inequalities, and therewith better solutions to these problems.

The Nature of the Sample

This study centers on graduate and undergraduate international students (i.e., non-immigrant foreign students) attending U.S. universities. Graduate students were selected because their degrees — master's and doctorates — are the highest the educational system can formally bestow and thus carry high value in all societies. Undergraduate students were included in the study to see whether factors influencing graduate students' choices were also at work in the case of undergraduate students. This would allow us to detect what specific factors influence graduate student decisions and to identify more precisely whether these decisions occurred during the undergraduate experience or even earlier. Since we were interested in relatively stable field choices, the undergraduate sample was limited to juniors and seniors. In a study like ours, based on questionnaires and thus cross-sectional analysis, access to both graduate and undergraduate experiences offers a glimpse into the dynamics of field of study choices.

Ten universities representing various regions of the United States participated in the study. These universities were selected on the basis of their geographical distribution and their large enrollment of international stu-

8

dents.[2] With the collaboration of international student centers and scholar centers in these universities, a random sample of graduate and undergraduate international students was drawn. On the assumption that international students will constitute important change agents in their country of origin, the student sample was limited to international students from developing countries.

In order to permit not only the comparison of men and women but also independent quantitative analysis of women, more women than men were sampled. Data were collected during November 1988 and January 1989. In some cases, universities provided student lists from which the random sample was selected; in other cases, the universities selected the random sample and mailed the questionnaires directly to students. In the latter case, each of the participating universities received students questionnaires already placed in envelopes and ready to be mailed upon the placement of a label containing the student's name and address.

Each university was asked to provide 150 graduate students (100 female and 50 male) and 100 undergraduate students (75 female and 25 male). In the case of three universities, the number of graduate students and undergraduates had to be reversed because their international undergraduate population turned out smaller than anticipated. In the case of four universities, the required ratio had to be relaxed at the undergraduate level because fewer female than male international students go to study there as undergraduates.

The student response rate to the questionnaire, despite follow-ups in those universities where this was possible, was relatively low, ranging from 21% to 55% for undergraduates, and from 33% to 56% for graduate students. The response rate was highest among mid-western universities and lowest in the universities on the east and west coasts of the United States. The higher response rate among graduate than undergraduate students re-

---

[2]The participating universities were: Ohio State University, University of Minnesota, University of Georgia, Stanford University, Columbia University, University of California at Santa Cruz, Michigan State University, University of Texas at Austin, University of Wisconsin at Madison, and the University of Southern California. This sample includes the universities with the four largest foreign student populations (USC, University of Texas at Austin, Columbia University, and the University of Wisconsin at Madison). The sample also includes universities whose location attracts international students from various parts of the world. [According to IIE's *Open Doors* (1987), which was used to develop the criteria for university selection, Asian students are evenly distributed throughout the United States, but Latin American, African, and Middle Eastern students tend to concentrate in the south of the country. The midwest attracts many African and Middle Eastern students.] The University of California at Santa Cruz was not selected for having a large number of international students, which it does not have; it was included because of its wide reputation as an institution that attracts independent, creative minds.

9

flects perhaps a greater appreciation of research efforts at more advanced levels of education. The response rate, although low by conventional standards, is similar to that obtained in previous surveys of international students in the United States (see, for example, Zikopoulos and Barber, who report return rates ranging from 17% to 53%, 1986, pp. 3-4).

The sample consisted of 446 graduate students and 313 undergraduates. The distribution of students by gender and level of study is shown in **Table 1**.

Table 1
Distribution of Students in Sample by Level of Education and Gender

Graduate Students	Women	Men	Total
M.A.	48	5	53
M.S.	69	35	104
Ph.D.	173	85	258
Other	21	1	22
Did not identify degree	—	—	9
Total	311	126	446
Undergraduate Students			
B.A.	70	25	95
B.S.	117	81	198
Did not identify degree	—	—	20
Total	187	106	313

Although the response rate was modest, there is no reason to believe the sample was biased. The sampled students' distribution by source of funding and region of origin resembles those reported in the annual statistics of international students in the United States (*Open Doors*, 1989). Among the entire population of international students, 59% report that their studies are being supported either by their families or their own efforts and 21% are funded by the U.S. universities where they study (*Open Doors*, p. 36). The corresponding rates for the students in our sample are 57% and 29%.[3]

In terms of their region of origin, our sample reflects also the international student population. There is a slight tendency in our sample of underrepresentation of students from the Middle East and overrepresentation of Asian students **(Table 2)**.

The sampled students as a whole constitute a very homogeneous group,

[3]The number of those students who are funded by a U.S. university may be larger in our sample due to the larger number of graduate-level students we examined; many of these students obtain teaching or research assistantships.

Table 2

Comparison of the Population and Sample of International Students
by Region of Origin (Percentages)

	Population*	Grad. Stud.	Undergrad. Stud.
Latin America	15	15	13
Asia	63	73	69
Middle East	13	6	11
Africa	9	6	7
	100	100	100

* Source: IIE, 1989, p. 17

having parents with considerably greater levels of education than average
for their country of origin. Mothers had an average level of education equivalent to complete secondary, while fathers had an average level equivalent to incomplete higher education. In terms of occupational status (which
will be explained later), the parents had high scores, with fathers averaging
a rating of 80 and mothers an average rating of 76 (on a scale which ranged
from 0 to 98 points).

Techniques of Data Gathering

A questionnaire was developed and field tested during the summer of 1988.
Approximately 20 graduate and undergraduate international students (10
in each category) took part in field testing, which included answering the
questionnaire and then participating in in-depth interviews to detect whether the questions had been understood and captured the various experiences and attitudes that were pertinent. Following field testing, a number
of changes were made, particularly in the wording of certain items.

Questionnaires were mailed to the students in October 1988 with an intro-
ductory letter and a self-addressed stamped envelope. The instruments for
graduate and undergraduate students were similar, except that in the case
of graduate students questions addressing their experience in academic
capacities within their departments and their married life were included. The
undergraduate students' questionnaire comprised 83 items; that of the
graduate students, 88 items. The questionnaires used in this study appear
in **Appendix A** (graduate students) and **Appendix B** (undergraduates).

The questionnaire took about 25 to 35 minutes to answer. This probably dissuaded some of the students in the sample. But the long questionnaire was
a deliberate choice on the part of the researcher, who preferred greater
depth of information to a larger sample with fewer aspects probed. While
the questionnaire was long, there is no evidence that those who responded

to it were affected by fatigue. This can be discerned from the high number of responses to the feminism scale in the questionnaire, which was the last item. There were only 24 missing responses to this scale in the sample of graduate students and 14 in the undergraduates.

Field of study choice, the key dependent variable in this study, was examined according to two definitions, each involving a separate analysis. The first definition considered field of study in a nominal way, looking at fields according to well-established classifications of higher education fields. This definition utilized a modified version of the 18 categories employed in UNESCO statistics of higher education (see for example, UNESCO, 1986), producing a list of 12 categories. Other classifications of fields, such as the classification of instructional programs produced by the U.S. National Center for Education Statistics, while excellent, were considered less appropriate because they combine academic disciplines and vocational skills in their classification. The distribution of the graduate and undergraduate students in the sample according to the UNESCO-based classification is shown in **Table 3**.

Table 3
Distribution of Student Sample by Category of Field of Study
and Level of Study

Field	Graduates		Undergraduates	
	Women	Men	Women	Men
Managerial	18	10	54	15
Technological Fields	35	46	46	64
Exact Sciences	45	18	10	6
Agricultural Fields	9	5	3	5
Medicine and Biological Sciences	48	10	34	5
Social and Behavioral Sciences	110	27	24	11
Home Economics	4	—	2	—
Humanities	26	5	5	1
Fine and Applied Arts	7	—	13	—
Communications	6	—	6	1
Law	2	—	—	—
Architecture	—	3	5	3
Total	315	126	202	111

These categories were used in analyses that contrasted students located at the poles of conventional and nonconventional fields. In this polarization, management, technology, the exact sciences, and agriculture were defined as masculine fields (i.e., nonconventional for women) and home economics, the humanities, and fine and applied arts were defined as feminine fields (i.e., conventional for women).

While the nominal classification was found to represent accurately dominant social definitions of conventional and nonconventional fields for women, there are two reasons why it was not very efficient for the purposes of subsequent multiple variable analysis: (1) it excluded some fields from the analysis; and (2) it treated fields as binary choices, when, in fact, it could be argued that the notion of conventional fields covers a continuum with more points of differentiation. In consequence, field of study choices were also defined according to a five-point scale, ranging from a field considered extremely conventional for women (0) to a field extremely nonconventional for women (4).

The development of this conventionality scale used criteria previously utilized in the definition of male dominated occupations (Bridges and Bower, 1985), stereotypes concerning men and women's differences and preferences (Deaux, 1984; Reskin and Hartmann, 1986), and descriptions of occupations offered in pre-women's movement guidance books (see for example Hardy and Cull, 1974). Also considered in the development of the conventionality scale was the notion (offered by Bryant, 1972) that the sexual division of labor is affected by both a space sex and a tool sex reference; in other words, jobs and occupations allocated by gender are associated with certain locales or settings and the use of certain tools and equipment.

In this scale, degree of conventionality was measured in additive fashion, granting one point for each of the following features of a field of study:

1. It involves leadership skills and managing people, as opposed to caring, supportive, and nurturing attitudes.
2. It involves physical strength and danger or risk in everyday activities.
3. It requires natural sciences and math skills.
4. It involves working away from home or being frequently away from home so that it conflicts with family life.

If none of these qualities was present, the field was assigned a score of 0.

For the development of this scale, each of the graduate students' specializations was first classified within a broad academic category and field of study. In cases where there was uncertainty regarding the classification of the field or specialization, the most relevant faculty or department in the University of Southern California was consulted to get a precise understanding of the features of the specialization. All together, a total of 12 major disciplines, 112 fields of study, and 280 specializations were identified. The complete list of academic categories, fields of study, and specializations appears in **Appendix C**. This list also presents the conventionality score of each field and specialization.

The scoring of the various specializations was conducted by a two-person team that assessed each specialization according to the criteria identified above. This team was composed of the researcher (knowledgeable about educational systems and gender conditions, particularly in Latin America and Africa) and one of the research assistants, an M.A. graduate with considerable knowledge and experience in education and social communications in Latin America. All scores represented the consensual views of the two judges.

Since our theoretical framework defines the selection of a nonconventional field as a form of social defiance, we hypothesized that students going into those fields would score high on a scale of feminism. Since many of the existing gender/feminist scales emphasize psychological preferences or abstract attitudes that often seem closely bound to U.S. culture, we developed a scale more applicable to international students. The scale focused on specific trends of behavior in the sphere of family, work, and social relations. It underwent wide testing during the pilot phase of the questionnaire. On the basis of the pilot information, new items were developed and several which did not discriminate well were dropped. Thus a feminism scale was produced, which in its final version consisted of eight items. Items in this scale were scored from 1 to 4, the higher score indicating a stronger level of feminism. The reliability coefficient for this scale (Cronbach's alpha, a measure of internal consistency) was moderate. The scale produced a reliability coefficient of .63 among graduate students and .65 among undergraduates. The scale proved to be slightly more consistent among men than women (.68 for male and .62 for female graduate students, and .67 for male and .61 for female undergraduates). Yet the scale turned out to have strong predictive validity, as it consistently discriminated between male and female students, whether at the graduate or undergraduate level, and regardless of cultural affiliation (assessed by examining students from Asia, Africa, Latin America, and the Middle East as separate groups).

Methods of Analysis

Three types of comparisons are made in this study. First, international students are compared along gender lines, trying to see what the similarities and differences are in the process and experience of field selection due merely to gender and corresponding socialization. This provides the most basic comparison, that of gender differences across fields. Second, the study compares women who select conventional fields with women in nonconventional fields; this shows how individual preferences and capabili-

14

ties interact with field of study, holding gender constant. Third, the study compares women and men students in nonconventional fields, enabling us to understand how the two genders select and experience nonconventional fields. **Figure A** depicts the three comparisons (indicated through the boxed entries) conducted in the study. An analysis of the students by region of origin was considered beyond the scope of the study.

Figure A
Comparative Scheme for the Analysis of Field of Study Choices

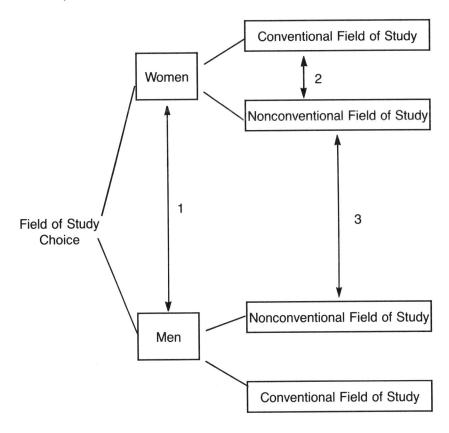

In addition to the comparisons indicated above, the study also tests empirically causal models of field of study choices. Two models are tested, one for graduate students and the other for undergraduates. These models are applied first to all students as a group (men and women) and then to women only.

For the comparisons between groups (i.e., men and women in general, women in nonconventional fields and women in conventional fields, men and women in nonconventional fields), analyses based on t-tests or chi-square tests are used.[4] For the causal model, the analysis is based on soft-modeling techniques (see Chapter V).

---

[4]Chi-square tests compare groups which are assumed to be independent and whose data are not truly numerical. This approach was considered appropriate for the first type of analysis, when fields were classified as nominal and when the distribution of the responses for various categorical and ordinal variables was examined. (For a more extensive dicussion of the chi-square test, see Siegel, 1965.) In a few cases, the tables presenting chi-square tests do not show the entire distribution of the data but only the most intensive categories (e.g., most liked and least liked features of a field, top reasons for selecting a field). The chi-square values refer to two-tail tests of significance.

III.
Field of Study Choices
Among Graduate Students

Differences Between Male and Female Graduate Students

Reasons for Selecting a Field of Study

Field selection was explored through a structured item asking the students to identify as many reasons as applied in their decision; a total of six reasons were offered to the respondents.

Some important differences exist between male and female graduate students in their reported reasons for selecting a field of study. **Table 4** shows three statistically significant differences between the genders. The most frequently identified reasons for selecting a field of study — by men and women — are the interest in the discipline and the field's potential for future employment. More women, however, are likely to endorse a field because of their interest in the discipline (74% of the women compared to 65% of the men). While more women indicated a preference for a field because of its intrinsic appeal, women like men (42% in both cases) consider an important feature of the selected field its potential usefulness for securing a job. More women tend to select fields whose admission criteria are seen as lenient.

The future occupation's potential for creating conflict with family demands is also a reason considered by a good number of female students; gender differences of a statistically significant nature do not emerge, but more women (9%) than men (6%) are sensitive to the job's presumed interference with family life. It is interesting to observe that a similar (though very small) number of male and female students declared they were in a field because of family expectations; this item shows no gender differences. In contrast, more men than women report being in a field because of the advice or direction of a funding agency: 17% men versus 11% women. This finding suggests that funding agencies behave differently toward men and women, a fact that we will explore in greater detail as we examine the differences between men and women in nonconventional fields.

Table 4

Reasons for Field Selection by Gender in Absolute and Relative Numbers

Reason	Women	Men	Chi-square
1. Field will lead to definite employment opportunities	132 (42)	53 (42)	0
2. It is a field that will not create conflict with future family responsibilities	30 (9)	7 (6)	1.84
3. It is a field whose content interests me very much regardless of occupational potential	232 (74)	82 (65)	2.82*
4. The admission criteria for this field are not very rigorous	32 (10)	4 (3)	4.96**
5. My family expects me to enter this field	13 (4)	3 (3)	.78
6. Government or funding agency promoted the field	33 (11)	21 (17)	2.65*

   * Statistically significant at .10 level.
  ** Statistically significant at .05 level.
     Figures in parentheses denote percentages. The N is greater than the sample due to multiple responses for this item.

The selection of advanced fields of study among international students generally occurs before they come to this country, yet more women (28%) than men (19%) identify their fields once here (chi-square = 3.38, p = .06).[5] To understand how the graduate students came to know about the existence of their fields, they were asked an open-ended question: "How did you learn about your current field?" Responses to this item appear in **Table 5**.

Interesting differences emerge between men and women. Among women, the knowledge of their current field of studies is identified as having come

---

[5]A lower-case p here and throughout the text stands for the alpha probability level in statistical tests of significance.

18

Table 5
Sources of Awareness About Current Field of Study
in Absolute and Relative Numbers

Sources	Women (%)	Men (%)	Total (%)
Job experience	23 (16)	10 (23)	33 (17)
Readings:			
books and journals	14 (10)	2 (5)	16 (8)
career-related publications	1 (1)	2 (5)	3 (2)
university publications			
(catalogues, brochures)	3 (2)	—	3 (2)
Informal networks:			
friends/peers	20 (14)	4 (9)	24 (13)
professionals	4 (3)	1 (2)	5 (3)
Undergraduate study:			
coursework/seminars	55 (38)	21 (49)	76 (40)
professors	14 (10)	3 (7)	17 (9)
advisors	2 (1)	—	2 (1)
Family:			
parents/relatives	8 (5)	—	8 (4)
Media	2 (1)	—	2 (1)
Total	146 (101)*	43 (100)	189 (100)

* Percentage exceeds 100 due to rounding.

from informal networks (17% women versus 11% men). Men are more likely to find previous job experiences helpful (23%), as well as exposure to coursework, seminars, professors, and advisors during their undergraduate studies (56% men versus 49% women). The family as a source of awareness for the selected field of study is identified only by women, and it represents an infrequent source (identified only by 5% of the respondents).

Some conclusions from **Table 5** are that women rely more than men on informal networks for their information on different fields of study and that, as undergraduates, women tend to select a narrower range of courses, which prevents them from becoming acquainted with other fields and disciplines. To what extent enrollment in a few courses is a matter of choice as opposed to a consequence of not having the necessary prerequisites is an issue that will be discussed later in this study.

Likes and Dislikes Regarding Selected Fields

The students were asked to rank the three features of their fields they liked best and least. **Table 6** presents the differences between men and women in rating certain items as the most liked or the most disliked ones.

Table 6

Likes and Dislikes in Selected Field of Study

Likes	Women	Men	Chi-square
The discipline is of great interest to me	221 (70)	91 (72)	4.46
The discipline requires math/science skills	49 (16)	27 (21)	16.49**
The discipline requires verbal skills/English	25 (8)	4 (3)	5.26
The field offers many possibilities for finding a job	59 (19)	17 (14)	8.45
The field has a high prestige	31 (10)	13 (10)	7.89
I like its competitive atmosphere	30 (10)	8 (6)	6.73
The field is not dominated by one sex	32 (10)	2 (2)	27.83**
Dislikes			
The coursework is very difficult	37 (11)	14 (11)	6.34
The field offers few possibilities for finding a job	44 (14)	18 (14)	7.43
The field requires math/science skills	12 (4)	4 (3)	.98
The field requires verbal skills/English	25 (8)	11 (9)	5.59
The field has low prestige	27 (8)	7 (6)	5.69
I dislike its competitive atmosphere	46 (15)	13 (10)	6.13*
The field is dominated by one sex	33 (11)	13 (10)	1.73
There is nothing I dislike about my field	112 (35)	52 (41)	2.66

* Statistically significant at the .10 level.
** Statistically significant at the .05 level.
Figures in parentheses denote percentages.

Very few differences emerge between the genders in the features the students like best about their fields. Statistically significant differences appear regarding the math requirements of their disciplines, with a high math content being identified by more men than women as one of the most attractive features (21% men versus 16% women). Another statistically significant difference between men and women concerns the women's preference for a field that is not dominated by a single sex (10% women versus 2% men), which suggests that women are more sensitive to the gender composition of their fields than men.

There are almost no gender differences in terms of what students like least in their selected fields of study. Not surprisingly, the majority of the graduate students find very little to dislike in their specialization. The only dislike that shows a statistically significant difference is that more women (15%) than men (10%) dislike the competitive atmosphere of their field; indeed, this is the feature most disliked by the women.

The Role of Significant Others

Although 90% of the graduate students, both men and women, report that their field of study choice was almost exclusively made by themselves, the data suggest that this decision was influenced by a wide range of persons. The influence of significant others upon the decision of the students was measured by a 4-point Likert item that asked the respondent to rate the influence of a significant other along a continuum that ranges from not important to very important. Treating this variable as ordinal, the differences between men and women are presented in means, and t-test values are used to assess the levels of statistically significant differences.

According to **Table 7**, the most influential others in shaping the students' field of choice are professionals in the field. These social actors obtain a mean of 2.53, i.e., are identified as important and somewhat important in influencing the students' selection. The second most influential others are teachers. Parents are recognized as very influential by approximately 9% of the female and 7% of the male graduate students. When parents are recognized as very important persons in influencing field of study choices, fathers and mothers are mentioned more often by female than male students but these differences do not reach statistical significance. In this general comparison between men and women regarding the influence of significant others, no statistically significant gender differences emerge.

Table 7
Mean Level of Influence of Significant Others by Gender

Significant Other	Women	Men	T-test
Father	1.79 (1.02)	1.82 (1.03)	.32
Mother	1.69 (.94)	1.61 (.87)	−.86
Teacher/s	2.24 (1.04)	2.38 (.96)	1.22
School counselor	1.30 (.64)	1.34 (.63)	.47
Professionals in the field	2.53 (1.09)	2.53 (1.08)	.07
College peers	1.80 (.92)	1.76 (.89)	−.31
Relatives/siblings	1.41 (.79)	1.38 (.80)	−.40
Mass media	1.65 (.92)	1.76 (.99)	1.06

Figures in parentheses are standard deviations. If no level of significance is indicated here and in subsequent tables, the results are not significant.

About two-thirds of the graduate students report having received "messages" from significant others attempting to dissuade them from their current field of study. Men report receiving slightly more negative messages than women (78% versus 71%, producing a chi-square = 2.00, n.s). However, when asked to identify the sources of these messages and the reasons they offered for avoiding particular fields of study, 146 of the women (46%) but only 43 of the men (34%) could give or were willing to give the specifics.

Table 8 presents the negative messages concerning fields of study conveyed to women and men by type of reason given. It shows that only women are subject to negative messages related to their gender. In the case of women, 33% of the negative messages involve gender stereotypes prevail-

Table 8
Reasons Conveyed to Students to Deter Them
from Current Field of Study Choice

Reasons	Women	Men	Total
Job-related			
no job opportunity	18 (18)	15 (65)	33 (27)
low salary	17 (17)	3 (13)	20 (16)
loss of current job	1 (1)	—	1 (1)
job is too difficult	2 (2)	—	2 (2)
Study abroad			
culture shock	1 (1)	—	1 (1)
leaving country/going away from home	4 (4)	—	4 (3)
Adequacy to country's needs			
field irrelevant to country	4 (4)	1 (4)	5 (4)
Gender-related			
not suitable for women	11 (11)	—	11 (9)
conflict with marriage	3 (3)	—	3 (2)
conflict with family	7 (7)	—	7 (6)
too hard for women	2 (2)	—	2 (2)
no further studies needed	10 (10)	—	10 (8)
Academic reasons			
too demanding	6 (6)	2 (9)	8 (6)
low prestige	10 (10)	—	10 (8)
too long	1 (1)	1 (4)	2 (2)
too expensive	1 (1)	—	1 (1)
not challenging enough	1 (1)	1 (4)	2 (2)
hostility to field	1 (1)	—	
Total	101 (100)	23 (99)	124 (102)

Figures in parentheses are percentages; in some cases the total exceeds or is smaller than 100 due to rounding. The absolute numbers are smaller than those in the total sample because many students did not reply to this open-ended item.

ing in society. They cover such reasons as: the field not being suitable for women; leading to a career that will conflict with marriage or family; involving a subject matter that is too hard for women; or simply that women have no need for further studies. Also, only in the case of women negative messages concern study abroad; these include the possibility of culture shock or the individual's going "far away from home." These latter reasons account for 5% of the negative messages.

In the case of men, most negative messages (78%) are related to future jobs, and the main reasons offered are that the field selected may lead to no employment, or that the salaries in the eventual occupations may be too low. Negative academic reasons are offered to both men and women (17% and 20%, respectively). Surprisingly, only women report being told that their selected fields may have low prestige. This reference to low prestige may be a veiled message that certain fields are not reputable for women.

Tables 9 and **10** identify the negative messages by source for women and men, respectively. Among women, negative messages are frequently received from family (from parents, fathers, mothers, and relatives), accounting for 41% of negative sources. Second in frequency are the negative messages coming from the informal network of friends, boyfriends, and peers (33% of negative sources). School sources (teachers, advisors, and professionals) are also identified as providing negative messages; the number of these messages, although smaller than in the case of family and friends, is still substantial, 13% of all negative messages.

Among men, the family also produces negative messages regarding field of study choices, but they are less frequent (33%). In contrast, the informal network of friends produces a larger number of negative messages (50%), while school sources are slightly larger in number (17%) than those producing negative messages for women. The fact that the negative sources of messages for women derive from the family while those for men derive from the informal networks of friends suggests that women are subjected to more intense and repeated messages, because family contacts are certainly stronger and more constant than those with outsiders.

The previous data indicate that although individuals may feel that their field of study choice is their own, such a choice evolves after initial choices are eliminated through the guidance and expectations of others. Further support for this assertion is provided by the finding that a large number of students (52% of women and 42% of men; chi-square = 2.76, p = <.09) acknowledge having been interested in other advanced programs of study before making their choice. Given the wide array of actors providing messages about fields of study choice, it is likely that these actors often succeed in making the students abandon their initial field selection. Considering the

Table 9
Reasons Conveyed to Female Students to Deter Them from Current Field of Study Choice

Reasons	Source of Message													Total
---	P	M	F	R	ML	H	CH	BF	FR	PE	A	T	PR	---
Job-related														42 (35)
job opportunity	3			3					10	2			3	21
low salary			1	6					5	2	1	1	3	18
loss of job									1					1
difficult job				1								1		2
Study abroad														6 (5)
culture shock				1					1					2
leaving country/away from home	1		1	1			1							4
Adequacy to country's needs														3 (2)
field irrelevant to country				2					1					3
Gender-related														46 (38)
not suitable for women	3	2	1	7					2				4	19
conflict with marriage		1			1	1								3
conflict with family	2			3		2	1		2				2	12
too hard for a woman			1	1					1					3
no further study needed	2	2	1	1		1		1	1					9
Academic reasons														23 (19)
too demanding	1		1	2					2	1				7
low prestige		1		4					5	2				12
too long	1													1
too expensive	1													1
not challenging enough	1													1
hostility to field												1		1
Ethnic stereotype										1				1
													Total	121 (99)

Note: P = parents, M = mother, F = father, R = relatives, ML = mother in law, H = husband, CH = children, BF = boyfriend, FR = friend, A = advisor, T = teacher, PE = peer, PR = professional in field. Figures in parentheses denote percentages.

Table 10

Reasons Conveyed to Male Students to Deter Them from Current Field of Study Choice

Reasons	P	M	F	R	ML	H	CH	BF	FR	PE	B	A	T	PR	Total
Job-related															
job opportunity	1	—	—	1	—	—	—	—	3	5	1	1	1	1	14
low salary	2	—	—	1	—	—	—	—	1	—	—	—	—	—	4
loss of job	—	—	—	—	—	—	—	—	—	—	—	—	—	—	1
difficult job	—	—	—	—	—	—	—	—	—	—	—	—	—	—	1
Study abroad															18 (75)
culture shock	—	—	—	—	—	—	—	—	—	—	—	—	—	—	—
leaving country/away from home	—	—	—	—	—	—	—	—	—	—	—	—	—	—	—
Adequacy to country's needs															
field irrelevant to country	—	—	—	—	—	—	—	—	—	—	—	—	1	—	1 (4)
Gender-related	—	—	—	—	—	—	—	—	—	—	—	—	—	—	—
Academic reasons															
too demanding	—	—	—	—	—	—	—	—	2	—	—	—	—	—	2
low prestige	1	—	—	1	—	—	—	—	—	—	—	—	—	—	2
too long	—	—	—	—	—	—	—	—	—	—	—	—	—	—	—
too expensive	—	—	—	—	—	—	—	—	—	1	—	—	—	—	1
not challenging enough	—	—	—	—	—	—	—	—	—	—	—	—	—	—	—
hostility to field	—	—	—	—	—	—	—	—	—	—	—	—	—	—	—
Ethnic stereotype	—	—	—	—	—	—	—	—	—	—	—	—	—	—	5 (21)
														Total	24 (99)

Note: P = parents, M = mother, F = father, R = relatives, ML = mother in law, H = husband, CH = children, BF = boyfriend, FR = friend, B = boss, A = advisor, T = teacher, PE = peer, PR = professional in field.
Figures in parentheses denote percentages.

negative messages women receive, it is quite possible that the fields discarded by them were nonconventional fields of study. This possibility, unfortunately, was not probed in the questionnaire.

That the selection of a field of study is the result of a long process of social experiences, in which the influence of significant others shape understandings of acceptable work and gender roles, is further supported by the finding that over 21% of male and 24% of female students report no specific preparation immediately prior to the selection of their field of study. Among the 25% of students who do prepare for their choice, significant differences appear along gender lines. Men prepare more than women by reading books. Women tend to prepare by talking to teachers or professionals in their selected fields. Again, this corroborates the importance of informal, oral communication channels for women, as well as their special need for wider social networks.

The Presence of Role Models

The majority of graduate students report having role models in their fields (59% women and 54% men), and the difference along gender lines is not statistically significant. Interestingly, for both genders this role model is a person usually identified after the field of study is selected (see **Table 11**).

Table 11

Presence and Time of Identification of Role Models by Gender

| | Women | | Men | | Chi- |
	Yes	No	Yes	No	square
Reports an adult whom student considers an example to follow	186 (59)	128 (41)	67 (54)	58 (46)	.94
Role model prior to choice of field	67 (35)	125 (65)	28 (41)	41 (59)	.48

Strong and statistically significant differences emerge in the gender of the role model vis-a-vis the gender of the students: most students have a male role model but female students much more often report a female role model

Table 12

Gender of Role Model by Gender of the Graduate Student

	Women	Men
Female role model	72 (38)	4 (6)
Male role model	115 (62)	64 (94)
	187 (100)	68 (100)

Chi-square = 23.82; statistically significant at the .05 level.
Figures in parentheses represent percentages.

(38% of female, in contrast with 6% of male students; see **Table 12**). The substantial number of female role models among women probably reflects a tendency in all individuals to be inspired by those with whom they share some features in common. For women, it is possible that seeing other women in successful positions is such an inspiring experience.

The fact that the role model emerges after the selection of field of study does not necessarily diminish its importance; it may be that the presence of the role model has an impact primarily on the individuals' persistence in their selected field. We shall try to verify this potentially important effect in a later section.

Views of Gender in Society

According to our theoretical framework, an important factor in the process of field of study choice is the students' understanding of the conditions of gender in society and their own level of feminist awareness. It is hypothesized that greater understanding of gender inequalities in society will lead female students to challenge dominant preconceptions of what are appropriate fields for women. It is also hypothesized that more female than male students will tend to be aware of gender inequities and that levels of feminism will be higher among women than men.

The students' view of gender in society was assessed through a three-item forced response asking them to select the response that most closely resembles conditions in their home country. These responses ranged from the perception that women held extremely disadvantageous positions compared to men to the belief that conditions were now equal for both genders. The responses to these items were scored according to the degree of perceived equality, so that 1 was given if substantial inequalities affecting women were perceived, 2 if mild inequalities were observed, and 3 if substantial equality was perceived. Three areas of equality were explored: occupational conditions, educational attainment, and educational treatment by teachers. (In the case of educational attainment, the range was four points, with 4 being the score for total equality.)

In examining the views of male and female graduate students in general (**Table 13**), we find a tendency on the part of both genders to hold a rather naive view of the condition of women in their country. They see their societies as harmonious: societies in which women suffer little or no discrimination either in the labor force or in education since both of them are equal in jobs and men and women have the same levels of education. Likewise, they believe that the educational system expects the same performance from boys and girls. No statistically significant differences emerge between the mean of these two groups, though men do manifest a stronger tendency toward seeing no gender inequalities in society.

Table 13
Views of Gender Conditions in Country of Origin by Gender

View	Women	Men	T-test
Equality of gender in the labor market	2.15 (.63)	2.19 (.64)	.63
Equality of school attainment	3.27 (1.10)	3.40 (1.00)	1.13
Expectations of teachers toward men and women	2.33 (.87)	2.37 (.81)	.39

Figures in parentheses are standard deviations.

Probing further how perceptions of gender differences affect graduate students' selection of field of study, we asked the students whether they anticipated career/family conflicts in the future and how these might be solved. As shown in **Table 14**, it is clear that more men (54%) than women (41%) expect no conflicts. Confirming theoretical expectations, of those who anticipate family conflicts, more women (46%) than men (32%) anticipate that family considerations will prevail in the solutions to these conflicts. Overall, there are strong and statistically significant differences regarding what men and women students expect in the future. For women, the relegation of career to a lower priority than family responsibilities is seen as unavoidable and, possibly, unquestionable.

Table 14
Expectations Concerning Family and Career Conflict by Gender

Expectations	Women	Men
No conflict anticipated	119 (41)	63 (54)
There will be conflicts but family needs will take precedence	134 (46)	37 (32)
There will be conflicts but career needs will take precedence	38 (13)	16 (14)
	291 (100)	116 (100)

Chi-square = 7.32; d.f. = 2; statistically significant at .02.
Figures in parentheses denote percentages.

Marriage is the social institution with the greatest disruptive power in the attainment of professional occupational goals for women. Therefore, we examined how unmarried graduate students envisaged their future decisions if clear conflicts should emerge between spouse (a proxy for family situation) and career. No gender differences are revealed regarding the students' choice between marriage and career: most of the single graduate students (68% women versus 67% men) intend to marry. Also, most in both groups are confident that they will be able to change their spouses' mind should they oppose the idea of working outside the home and that they can bring about these changes before marrying their spouses (**Table 15**).

While no gender differences emerge in students' options regarding marriage and spouse's attitudes, it is interesting to observe that fewer men students (50%) than women (62%) answered this question. It is likely that the item made no sense to several men since it presents a condition that is problematic only for women.

Table 15
Options of Unmarried Students if Spouse
Is Opposed to Work After Marriage

Options	Women	Men
Choose marriage and forget career	6 (3)	2 (3)
Choose marriage and hope that spouse will change mind after marriage	19 (10)	6 (10)
Choose marriage and try to change future spouse's mind before marriage	106 (55)	34 (54)
Choose career and forget marriage	61 (32)	21 (33)

Chi-square = .056; d.f. = 3; n.s.
Figures in parentheses denote percentages.

For female students who were married, the levels of anticipated spouse support were much more modest than for married male students (**Table 16**). Men anticipated much more spouse support for their careers much more frequently than women did (48% men versus 26% women). While married female students did anticipate support from their current spouses, a large

Table 16
Degree of Support from Spouse for Future Career

Type of Support	Women	Men
Very supportive of my career; spouse will, if necessary, give priority to job demands regarding location, schedules, and travel	32 (26)	29 (48)
Very supportive of my career, but spouse's own career demands take priority	41 (33)	4 (7)
Very supportive of my career; all career moves between us have equal weight	44 (35)	23 (38)
Not very supportive of my career demands; sometimes this is a source of conflict at home	6 (5)	4 (7)
Not at all supportive of my career; sometimes this undermines my career	2 (2)	1 (2)
	125 (100)	61 (100)

Chi-square = 17.99, d.f. = 4; statistically significant at the .001 level.

29

number of these women (33%) also realized that their husbands' careers will take priority over their own. In contrast, only 7% of male graduate students anticipated that their wives' careers would take precedence.

Knowledge of Feminism and Feminism Score

Only 6% of women and 9% of men considered themselves as "very knowledgeable" of women's issues. The mean value for men and women is modest, (2.40 and 2.49, respectively) ranging from being "somewhat knowledgeable" to "not very knowledgeable" (**Table 17**).

For those who declared they knew something, no gender differences emerge regarding the impact of newspapers and TV programs on their understanding of women's issues, but significant differences do exist regarding the impact of both general coursework and courses dealing with gender issues. These differences indicate that coursework exerts a weak influence on men but a rather strong influence on women. Further, for women the role of informal conversations is important in spreading knowledge about gender issues and surpasses the influence attributed to either type of coursework. Although participation in feminist groups is generally identified as a rather weak source of knowledge about gender issues, it is significantly less important for male than female students. The reason for the low impact attributed to participation in feminist groups appears to be that few international students participate in them. We know this not on the basis of data from the questionnaire but rather from observations of campus activities and comments made by faculty in women's studies in several U.S. universities.

Table 17

Knowledge and Sources of Information about Gender Issues by Gender

	Women	Men	T-test
Knowledge of women's issues	2.49 (.73)	2.40 (.82)	−1.01
Source of Knowledge:			
Newspapers	3.37 (.72)	3.41 (.68)	.29
TV	3.11 (.91)	3.00 (.87)	−.84
General courses at univ.	2.30 (1.09)	1.70 (.87)	−3.85**
Women's courses at univ.	2.36 (1.21)	1.90 (1.06)	−2.21**
Informal conversations	3.03 (.91)	2.62 (1.07)	−2.69**
Participation in feminist groups	2.01 (1.05)	1.65 (.91)	−1.69**

**Statistically significant at the .05 level or below.
Figures in parentheses are standard deviations.

There is a strong difference between female and male students in the degree to which they hold feminist beliefs. On all items in **Table 18**, women

30

are significantly more progressive than men. Women are less progressive than men only with regard to the belief that a woman should be as free as a man to propose marriage.

Table 18
Total Scale and Item Means in Feminism Scale by Gender

Item	Women	Men	T-test
1. Because of past discrimination against women in many kinds of jobs, they should be given preference over equally qualified men.	2.17 (1.05)	2.00 (1.04)	−1.45
2. A woman should be as free as a man to propose marriage.	3.24 (.90)	3.49 (.69)	3.08**
3. A woman should not expect to go to exactly the same places or to have quite the same freedom of action as a man.	3.27 (.95)	3.02 (.98)	−2.41**
4. In general, the father should have greater authority than the mother in bringing up the children.	3.47 (.84)	2.96 (1.00)	−4.91**
5. A married woman should not accept a job that requires her to be away from home overnight.	2.95 (1.06)	2.20 (1.04)	−6.67**
6. Certain jobs should be done by women and certain jobs should be done by men.	2.64 (1.08)	2.08 (1.01)	−4.96**
7. Wife and husband should share the economic responsibility of supporting a family.	3.64 (.62)	3.20 (.74)	−5.83**
8. Women with small and school-age children should not work outside the home unless absolutely necessary.	2.85 (1.01)	2.28 (.93)	−5.62**
Total Scale	24.24 (3.82)	21.26 (4.05)	−7.09**

**Statistically significant at the .05 level.

Summary

The comparison of men and women graduate students shows that women tend to select fields of study primarily because of an interest in the discipline *per se*. Comparison also shows that men prefer fields of study that emphasize math and science, while women prefer fields that do not have rigorous entry criteria. During the quite lengthy time when choices develop, parents and family members play a significant role in guiding the individual. Messages from parents and relatives probably encourage young people's choices most of the time; yet there is substantial evidence that many women receive advice that steers them away from nonconventional fields. In many of these cases, the justification for this advice is that the future occupation will conflict with established feminine responsibilities for family and household.

Regarding their view of gender issues in society, both men and women graduate students — despite their high levels of education and their presumed understanding of their social milieu — have a rather naive view of society, believing that there are no major gender problems. Women tend to have a slightly less naive view of gender conditions, and their scores in feminism are higher than those of men. Unfortunately, women do not translate these views into more progressive family and career roles; they anticipate — whether married or single — that family needs will take precedence over their careers.

Women in Nonconventional and Conventional Fields

We now move on to a close comparison of women in nonconventional fields (NCF hereafter) with those in conventional fields (CF). NCF are those traditionally defined as masculine. They include the fields of management, technology, the exact sciences, and agriculture. CF are home economics, the humanities, and the fine and applied arts. For the purposes of this comparison, fields that fall in the middle of the spectrum (i.e., medicine and biological sciences, social and behavioral sciences, communications, law, and architecture) were excluded.

In undertaking this comparison, we are particularly interested in identifying the extent to which women in NCF follow a trajectory different from women in CF, and whether they display more progressive attitudes than women in CF. As explained earlier, if we found more progressive or egalitarian attitudes among women in NCF, this would show that the process of selecting this type of field is supported by strong beliefs in greater gender equality in society. Also, the presence of such progressive attitudes would allow us to expect that these university graduates will become agents for change as they enter the labor force and other sectors of society.

Reasons for Selecting a Field of Study

More similarities than differences emerge between the reasons women in NCF and CF choose their fields. Of the seven reasons for selecting a field of study, only one (an important one) produces a statistically significant difference: many more women in NCF stated that they chose their field because it definitely would lead to employment opportunities. The women in NCF seem, then, especially attentive to market forces.

Table 19

Reasons for Field Selection by NCF and CF Women
in Absolute and Relative Numbers

Reason	NCF Women	CF Women	Chi-square
1. Field will lead to definite employment opportunities	59 (55)	12 (32)	5.32*
2. It is a field that will not create conflict with future family responsibilities	11 (10)	1 (3)	1.27
3. It is a field whose content interests me very much regardless of occupational potential	78 (73)	29 (76)	.84
4. The admission criteria for this field are not very rigorous	12 (12)	4 (11)	0
5. My family expects me to enter this field	6 (7)	2 (5)	0
6. Government or funding agency promoted the field	8 (5)	2 (5)	0

*Statistically significant at the .05 level.

We saw earlier that the majority of women students select their fields for advanced studies before they come to this country. But a larger number of women in NCF select their fields only **after** coming to this country (57% of the NCF vs. 31% of the CF women, producing a chi-square of 5.70, p = .01). Apparently, the social and academic environment in the United States encourages the selection of nonconventional fields by women who have the necessary prerequisites. We are unsure about the mechanisms — professors, peers, content of courses, extracurricular activities — that may operate here.

Likes and Dislikes concerning NCF and CF

In terms of what they like best about their field, the major difference between women in CF and NCF is that the latter like their fields because they require math and science skills, and the former like their fields because they require verbal/English skills; both differences are strong and statistically significant. Other differences between the two groups are the following: many more CF women consider the prestige of their field a highly important feature; again, the majority in CF like the competitive nature of the field; more women in CF than NCF like their field not to be dominated by one sex.

These findings are surprising in that we would have expected NCF women to identify the competitive atmosphere and the prestige of their field among the best liked features. Traditional male occupations carry more prestige than feminine occupations and tend to be more competitive in terms of the organizational structures in which they operate. Perhaps what is at work in the women's perception of high prestige in their fields is that women are socialized into believing that traditional occupations for women are "proper" and, by extension, better regarded by others — hence the prestige. The preference of CF women for fields that are not dominated by one sex is somewhat ambiguous but it could mean that CF women do not want to be in fields dominated by men.

Concerning the features they dislike most in their respective fields, no differences emerge between the two groups of women.

Table 20
Likes and Dislikes of Women in NCF and CF in Their Selected Field of Study

Likes	NCF	CF	Chi-square
The discipline is of great interest to me	66 (62)	31 (82)	6.43*
The discipline requires math/science skills	27 (25)	2 (2)	36.00**
The discipline requires verbal skills/ English	4 (4)	8 (21)	23.13**
The field offers many possibilities for finding a job	26 (24)	5 (13)	6.82
The field has a high prestige	8 (8)	10 (26)	11.34**
I like its competitive atmosphere	9 (8)	9 (24)	6.90**
The field is not dominated by one sex	6 (6)	9 (24)	16.56**
Dislikes			
The coursework is very difficult	10 (9)	8 (21)	5.44
The field offers few possibilities for finding a job	14 (13)	11 (29)	5.97
The field requires math/science skills	12 (2)	2 (5)	1.88
The field requires verbal skills/ English	6 (6)	2 (5)	2.49
The field has low prestige	2 (2)	4 (11)	5.92
I dislike its competitive atmosphere	21 (20)	6 (16)	4.22
The field is dominated by one sex	13 (12)	2 (5)	1.48
There is nothing I dislike about my field	45 (42)	8 (21)	5.65

  * Statistically significant at the .10 level.
 ** Statistically significant at the .05 level or below.
    Figures in parentheses indicate percentages.

The Role of Significant Others

In the comparison between male and female graduate students, no differences emerge in the influence of significant others upon the selection of field. However, between women in conventional and nonconventional fields, two significant others appear to have different amounts of influence.

Table 21

Mean Level of Influence of Significant Others Among NCF and CF Women

Significant Other	NCF	CF	T-test
Father	1.99 (1.08)	1.62 (.80)	−1.80*
Mother	1.85 (.96)	1.66 (.95)	1.02
Teacher/s	2.19 (1.02)	2.38 (1.01)	.96
School counselor	1.31 (.62)	1.43 (.62)	.88
Professionals in the field	2.24 (1.02)	2.72 (1.15)	2.25*
College peers	1.80 (.95)	1.88 (.84)	.41
Relatives/siblings	1.49 (.85)	1.28 (.72)	−1.26
Mass media	1.53 (.86)	1.46 (.76)	−.37

* Statistically significant at the .05 level.
Figures in parentheses are standard deviations.

The father plays an influential role in the selection of nonconventional fields; 28% of women in NCF identify him as "very important" or "important" compared to only 5% in CF. It should be noted that in our sample most fathers were highly educated; thus, educated fathers seem to play a progressive influence on daughters, contrary to what has been observed among low-educated fathers. The influence of the mother as "very important" or "important" is reported by similar proportions of respondents (19% of the NCF and 17% of the CF women) and does not reach statistical significance. Differences between the two groups of women appear in the influence of professionals in the selection of field of study. This influence is less noticeable in the selection of nonconventional fields, which suggests that professionals in nonconventional fields may be playing a rather conservative role in the orientation of women into careers, or that professionals in nonconventional fields are not easily available to many female students. The influence of professionals in the field upon the selection of CF is by far the strongest of all; this suggests that it will be difficult for many women to move into NCF as long as the majority of professionals available to them are in CF. If only professionals in traditional fields are available to women, they are likely to encourage women to go into their fields.

Compared to the preparation reported by male and female students in general, women in CF speak much more often to professionals than women in NCF. Significantly, more women in nonconventional fields (33% in NCF vs. 14% of those in CF) report having engaged in no specific preparation for their fields. This finding suggests again that selection of nonconventional fields is a long, cumulative process of including and excluding certain disciplines as not proper or productive.

35

The Presence of Role Models

Approximately 50% of all female students report having role models. Women in NCF report fewer role models (49%) than women in CF (63%), but this difference does not reach statistical significance (**Table 22**). As in the comparison of male and female graduates, the identification of role models follows the selection of field. This occurs in 76% of the cases, regardless of whether the women are in conventional or nonconventional fields.

Table 22

Presence and Time of Identification of Role Models Among NCF and CF

| | NCF | | CF | | Chi-square |
	Yes	No	Yes	No	
Reports an adult whom student considers an example to follow	52 (49)	55 (51)	24 (63)	24 (37)	1.83
Role model prior to choice of field	13 (24)	42 (76)	6 (24)	19 (76)	0

Women in CF report more female role models than those in NCF, not a surprising finding given the predominance of male faculty and researchers in NCF (**Table 23**).

Table 23

Gender of Role Model by NCF and CF Women

	NCF	CF
Female role model	159 (28)	16 (67)
Male role model	38 (72)	8 (33)
	53 (100)	24 (100)

** Statistically significant at the .05 level.

  Figures in parentheses represent percentages.

We hypothesized earlier that while role models do not play a significant role in leading individuals to select a particular field of study, they may help students to stay in their selected fields, particularly when these fields go counter to established social expectations. This question is illuminated by comparing the presence and gender of role models among master's and Ph.D. students across types of fields.

As shown in **Table 24**, more NCF women at the Ph.D. level (61%) report role models than at the master's level (34% for the M.A. and M.S. combined). The data show that, in fact, female students have more role models as they continue into more advanced studies. Among CF women, the increase is from 56% at the master's level to 71% at the doctoral level. Among

NCF women, there is also an increase, from 34% at the master's level to 61% at the doctoral level. Moreover, as women move to more advanced degrees, the number who report a female role model increases. Among CF women, female role models increase from 56% to 73%; among NCF women, the increase goes from 13% to 31%. In other words, CF women increase their female role models by less than half, while NCF women increase their female role models by a factor of 2.3. This finding tends to support theoretical expectations about the importance of like-sex role models for staying in nonconventional fields. However, this is not a universal experience, because almost half of the NCF women report not having a role model at all (see **Table 22**).

Table 24
Presence and Gender of Role Model by Level of Study
and Type of Field (in Percentages)

	NCF Women		CF Women	
	M.A./M.S.	**Ph.D.**	**M.A.**	**Ph.D.**
Reports an adult whom the student considers an example to follow	34	61	56	71
Has female role model	13	31	56	73

Although the majority of role models among NCF women are men, this may well be a function of the scant presence of women as professors and professionals in nonconventional fields. If this is indeed the case, it could be argued that it is rather extraordinary that NCF women select so many female role models when only 3% of the males in these fields report a female role model (see **Table 35**). The presence of people whose key attributes one shares (i.e., gender identification leading to similar societal expectations, similar family constraints, etc.) must operate as a powerful source of comfort and inspiration.

Views of Gender in Society

Female students as a group tend to hold rather naive or unrealistic views of the conditions of women in their country; thus, they believe that women there face no discrimination in the labor market or in schooling. And, against theoretical expectations, NCF women have even a slightly more naive view than CF women, (see **Table 25**) though these differences fail to reach statistical significance. This naivete of NCF women does not predict a particularly progressive performance on their part were they to become national leaders upon their return to their country of origin.

Table 25

Views of Gender Conditions in Country of Origin by Women in NCF and CF

View	NCF	CF	T-test
Equality of gender in the labor market	2.15 (.62)	1.92 (.67)	−1.94
Equality of school attainment	3.33 (1.02)	3.00 (1.31)	−1.58
Expectations of teachers toward men and women	2.39 (.90)	2.23 (.88)	− .90

Figures in parentheses are standard deviations.

With regard to anticipated career/family conflicts, more CF than NCF women expect such conflicts and fewer NCF (36%) than CF women (47%) expect no conflicts at all; we are unsure whether this reflects the CF women's confidence in asserting their rights in their future family situation or rather an optimistic view on their part. In so far as conflicts do occur, more NCF (17%) than CF women (11%) anticipate that their career will take precedence over family needs. These findings, however, fail to reach statistical significance.

Table 26

Expectations Concerning Family and Career Conflict
Among NCF and CF Women

	NCF	CF
No conflict anticipated	36 (36)	17 (47)
There will be conflicts but family needs will take precedence	47 (47)	15 (42)
There will be conflicts but career needs will take precedence	17 (17)	4 (11)
	100 (100)	36 (100)

Chi-square = 1.61; d.f. = 2; n.s.
Figures in parentheses denote percentages.

As in the comparison between male and female students, no significant differences emerge between NCF and CF women in terms of the career support they expect from future spouses. In both cases, the majority of students feel that they can change the spouse's objections to letting the wife work after marriage or that such persuasion can be successful before marriage. The findings show that the same proportion of NCF and CF women (36%) would choose a career and forego marriage if necessary. This finding is of interest because it reveals that women who pursue advanced studies have a strong commitment to their professional careers whether these are in conventional or nonconventional fields.

Table 27

Options of Unmarried NCF and CF Women
if Spouse Is Opposed to Work After Marriage

Option	NCF Women	CF Women
Choose marriage and forget career	3 (5)	0 (0)
Choose marriage and hope that spouse will change mind after marriage	5 (8)	4 (18)
Choose marriage and try to change future spouse's mind before marriage	34 (52)	10 (45)
Choose career and forget marriage	24 (36)	8 (36)
	66 (100)	22 (99)

Chi-square = 2.93; d.f. = 3; n.s.

The anticipated level of support from an actual spouse among the married students is significantly different between women in NCF and CF. No women in NCF expect little or no future support on the part of their husbands. Likewise, more NCF (38%) than CF women (24%) expect that their husbands will give equal weight to their own and their wives' careers. These two findings suggest greater egalitarianism in the households of NCF women. Yet the percentage of women who expect their husbands to give priority to the wife's career is the same and quite low, whether the graduate students are in nonconventional or conventional fields (18%). In other words, it would appear that the fact that women are in NCF does not frequently alter the balance of power within the household in their favor, even though there is a move toward greater equality (showing statistically significant differences) in their households than in those of CF women.

Table 28

Degree of Support from Spouse for Future Career
Among NCF and CF Women

Type of Support	NCF	CF
Very supportive of my career; spouse will, if necessary, give priority to job demands regarding location, schedules, and travel	7 (18)	3 (18)
Very supportive of my career, but spouse's own career demands take priority	17 (44)	7 (41)
Very supportive of my career; all career moves between us have equal weight	15 (38)	4 (24)
Not very supportive of my career demands; sometimes this is a source of conflict at home	0 (0)	3 (18)
Not at all supportive of my career; sometimes this undermines my career	0 (0)	0 (0)
	39 (100)	17 (101)

Chi-square = 7.67; d.f. = 4; statistically significant at the .05 level.

To assess further the degree of commitment of graduate-level women to their careers, we asked them to what extent they were likely to become involved in political and professional activities in their country. In general, these women expect to have very little political involvement. Against theoretical expectations, more women in NCF (77%) envisage little or no political involvement compared to 64% of the women in CF. The NCF women do anticipate more professional involvement (63%) than the women in CF (58%). In both cases, these differences are not statistically significant.

The similarity between NCF and CF women does not predict that NCF women will make political or professional contributions. Rather, their main contribution may be in increasing the representation of women in those professions.

Knowledge of Feminism and Feminist Score

As **Table 29** indicates, women in NCF exhibit a substantially lower level of knowledge regarding women's issues than CF women. When they are knowledgeable, their information comes primarily from the mass media (newspapers and TV). Women in NCF report getting less knowledge about gender issues from general courses, women's courses, or from participation in feminist groups (extracurricular activities) than CF women.

It is likely that NCF women tend to concentrate on their specialized courses and have little time for courses outside their specialization. This limited exposure of NCF women to knowledge of women's issues may account for their not being assertive in refusing future family constraints and thinking that gender inequalities in society are practically non-existent.

Table 29
Knowledge and Sources of Information About Gender Issues
Among NCF and CF Women

	NCF	CF	T-test
Knowledge of women's issues	2.25 (.71)	2.67 (.62)	3.14**
Source of Knowledge:			
Newspapers	3.40 (.57)	3.30 (.92)	−.55
TV	3.09 (.84)	3.22 (.86)	.60
General courses at univ.	1.59 (.73)	2.78 (1.13)	4.93**
Women's courses at univ.	1.74 (1.01)	2.57 (1.30)	2.67**
Informal conversations	2.85 (.95)	2.94 (1.07)	.33
Participation in feminist groups	1.60 (.85)	2.10 (1.15)	1.85*

  * Statistically significant at the .10 level.
 ** Statistically significant at the .05 level or below.
    Figures in parentheses are standard deviations.

On the feminism scale, no statistically significant differences emerge between CF and NCF women. It is interesting to observe, however, that CF women score higher than NCF women on 7 of the 8 scale items. The only statistically significant difference between the two groups indicates that women in CF are slightly more progressive, as they are more likely to believe that a woman may propose marriage to a man (see **Table 30**).

Table 30
Total Scale and Item Means in Feminism Scale of NCF and CF Women

Item	NCF	CF	T-test
1. Because of past discrimination against women in many kinds of jobs, they should be given preference over equally-qualified men	2.16 (1.08)	2.44 (1.13)	1.37
2. A woman should be as free as a man to propose marriage	3.06 (.98)	3.55 (.68)	3.31*
3. A woman should not expect to go to exactly the same places or to have quite the same freedom of action as a man	3.19 (.92)	3.35 (.88)	.91
4. In general, the father should have greater authority than the mother in bringing up the children	3.38 (.91)	3.43 (.89)	.30
5. A married woman should not accept a job that requires her to be away from home overnight	2.89 (1.06)	2.86 (1.21)	–.12
6. Certain jobs should be done by women and certain jobs should be done by men	2.58 (1.09)	2.81 (1.07)	1.11
7. Wife and husband should share the economic responsibility of supporting a family	3.55 (.69)	3.57 (.75)	.19
8. Women with small and school-age children should not work outside the home unless absolutely necessary	2.81 (1.03)	2.94 (1.08)	.63
Total Scale	23.69 (4.20)	25.00 (4.00)	1.64

* Statistically significant at the .05 level.

Summary

Altogether, NCF women tend to choose fields of study because these fields will lead to good employment opportunities and because these fields require skills in math and science, which the NCF women perceive themselves to have. Fathers emerge as influential figures in promoting the nonconventional choices of women, while professionals in the field influence mainly conventional choices.

NCF women do not see themselves as playing a role in the political or professional arena that is different from their CF colleagues. Their view of society, in fact, is more unrealistic or naive than the view of CF women, a consequence to a large extent of their narrow and demanding academic specialization, which translates into a sheltered existence vis-a-vis other dimensions of university and social life.

Women and Men in Nonconventional Fields

The purpose of this section is to explore whether individuals in nonconventional fields exhibit significant differences along gender lines, differences that would allow us to trace with greater predictive power the process of field selection and, subsequently, to predict more effectively different career and professional roles for men and women as they join the labor force.

Reasons for Selecting a Field of Study

Men and women who are in fields defined by society as being essentially masculine show relatively few statistically significant differences. The majority of female and male NCF students select their field because of an intrinsic interest in the discipline (73% of the women and 61% of the men). The employment-related rationale for selecting the field is more frequent among NCF women (55%) than men (43%). More women than men also report being in the field because the admission criteria are relatively easy, a fact that must be interpreted in light of the fact that the large number of women in nonconventional fields are strong in math and science. What women may mean, therefore, is that they find the admission criteria easy because they call for the quantitative skills they already possess.

We noted earlier that more men than women in general reported being in a field because of encouragement by a funding agency or their government. When we examine men and women in NCF, we find that more men (13%) than women (8%) are encouraged to move into particular nontraditional fields. These differences fail to reach statistical significance; yet they suggest that women are at a disadvantage when seeking financial support for moving into a nonconventional field.

Table 31

Reasons for Field Selection by Gender in Absolute and Relative Numbers

Reason	Women	Men	Chi-square
1. Field will lead to definite employment opportunities	59 (55)	34 (43)	2.66*
2. It is a field that will not create conflict with future family responsibilities	11 (10)	5 (6)	.49
3 It is a field whose content interests me very much regardless of occupational potential	78 (73)	48 (61)	2.53
4. The admission criteria for this field are not very rigorous	13 (12)	2 (3)	4.44**
5. My family expects me to enter this field	6 (6)	2 (3)	.43
6. Government or funding agency promoted the field	8 (8)	10 (13)	.86

* Statistically significant at .10 level.
** Statistically significant at .05 level.
Figures in parentheses denote percentages.

Continuing a pattern detected in earlier analyses, more women than men select their fields, particularly their nonconventional fields, after coming to the United States (29% of the women vs. 19% of the men). This difference, though sizable, falls slightly short of reaching the .10 level of statistical significance.

Likes and Dislikes within Nonconventional Fields

Regarding the likes and dislikes of students in NCF, a few statistically significant differences emerge. As **Table 31** shows, more men than women like their fields because they require math and science. More women than men like their fields for holding good possibilities for finding a job, which confirms the instrumental nature of NCF for many women. The majority of women also like the fact that their field is not "dominated by one sex." This item was also the best liked feature by women in CF. The apparently contradictory views that emerge (i.e., something being liked by both NCF and CF women) may be due to the possible ambiguity of the question, NCF women understanding it to mean similar representation of men and women as professionals in the field, CF women interpreting it as the absence of domination by men or women.

Table 32 shows that women in NCF dislike particularly the competitive nature of their field. This finding matches the emerging profile of NCF women: professionally committed women, very interested in their field, but not particularly concerned with aggressively asserting political or professional leadership roles.

Table 32

Likes and Dislikes About Selected Field of Study

Likes	Women	Men	Chi-square
The discipline is of great interest to me	66 (62)	54 (68)	1.23
The discipline requires math/science skills	27 (25)	23 (29)	6.43*
The discipline requires verbal skills/ English	4 (4)	4 (5)	.73
The field offers many possibilities for finding a job	26 (24)	10 (13)	10.75**
The field has a high prestige	8 (7)	9 (11)	1.50
I like its competitive atmosphere	9 (8)	5 (6)	2.10
The field is not dominated by one sex	7 (6)	2 (3)	7.80**

Dislikes			
The coursework is very difficult	10 (9)	11 (14)	3.54
The field offers few possibilities for finding a job	14 (13)	15 (19)	2.77
The field requires math/science skills	2 (2)	3 (4)	2.11
The field requires verbal skills/ English	6 (6)	6 (8)	.57
The field has low prestige	2 (2)	4 (5)	6.16
I dislike its competitive atmosphere	21 (20)	10 (13)	6.87*
The field is dominated by one sex	13 (12)	12 (15)	1.31
There is nothing I dislike about my field	2 (2)	3 (4)	1.93

  * Statistically significant at the .10 level.
 ** Statistically significant at the .05 level.
   Numbers in parentheses denote percentages.

The Influence of Significant Others

In the comparison of women and men in NCF, no substantial differences emerge regarding the influence of seven of the eight significant others they were asked about. Only the mother emerges as having more influence on women than men students; however, this influence is small and weaker than that of the father, of professionals in the field, and of teachers. Although few graduate students attributed an important influence to their mother, more NCF women (19%) than men (13%) consider the mother's influence of great significance. This suggests that for some few women, the existence of a close and constant source of support does lead to the choice of nonconventional fields.

The number of negative messages reported by women in nonconventional fields, as expected, clearly surpasses that reported by men; 54% of women

Table 33

Mean Levels of Influence of Significant Others by Gender

Significant Other	Women	Men	T-test
Father	1.99 (1.08)	1.85 (1.02)	−.82
Mother	1.81 (.96)	1.54 (.74)	−2.06*
Teacher/s	2.19 (1.02)	2.30 (1.07)	.69
School counselor	1.31 (.66)	1.30 (.55)	−.08
Professionals in the field	2.24 (1.02)	2.49 (1.08)	1.52
College peers	1.80 (.95)	1.75 (.90)	−.39
Relatives/siblings	1.49 (.85)	1.37 (.78)	−.93
Mass media	1.53 (.86)	1.78 (.96)	1.74

* Statistically significant at the 0.05 level.
  Figures in parentheses are standard deviations.

and 46% of men report having been discouraged. While this finding does not reach statistical significance, it suggests two facts: first, that women in nonconventional fields make choices that are often not supported by significant others; second, many women who are not in NCF may already have been successfully dissuaded, and, therefore, only appear to have "elected" to go into conventional fields of study.

Students report some degree of preparation for the selection of nonconventional fields, but a sizable number of respondents admit having taken no specific steps to gain knowledge about the field, either by reading books or talking to others about it, prior to making their decisions. A statistically significant difference by gender, however, appears among those who did not prepare themselves at all. More women (33%) than men (17%) admit no preparation at all. This finding reinforces our initial impression that a field of study choice — particularly the selection of a nonconventional field — is one that occurs over time. In view of the frequent messages women receive to avoid fields that will lead to disturbances in gender relations or norms, it is likely that women carefully examine the features of a field of study and that they develop strategies to pursue such a field. Such strategies probably involve a good deal of negotiation with, and in some cases avoidance of, significant others. These negotiations in turn are likely to be supported by factual data offered by the students as they try to convince others that their choices are sensible. Thus, women in NCF may need fortitude rather than formal preparation immediately preceding their field of study choices.

The Presence of Role Models

NCF students report fewer role models than students in general; likewise, they identify these models after the field of study was chosen. No gender differences emerge between NCF men and women in this regard (see Table 34). While the identification of the role model comes after the selection of field, its importance should not be minimized. It appears that a close role model is essential to the everyday experience of the students, since half of them acknowledge having such a role model.

Table 34
Presence and Time of Identification of Role Models by Gender

	Women		Men		Chi-
	Yes	No	Yes	No	square
Reports an adult whom student considers an example to follow.	52 (49)	55 (51)	35 (44)	44 (56)	.18
Role model prior to choice of field.	13 (24)	42 (76)	11 (30)	26 (70)	.16

Many more women than men in NCF (28% versus 3%) report having a female role model. The fact that women students tend to select female role models quite likely indicates that they identify more with persons who face similar social experiences, problems, and expectations.

Table 35
Gender of Role Model by Gender of the Graduate Students

	Women	Men
Female role model	15 (28)	1 (3)
Male role model	38 (72)	34 (97)
	53 (100)	35 (100)

Chi-square = 7.54, d.f. = 1; statistically significant at the .006 level.
Figures in parentheses represent percentages.

Views of Gender in Society

Concerning their appreciation of gender inequalities in society, students in NCF hold unrealistic views similar to those of their peers in other fields. No gender differences emerge among NCF students by gender (**Table 36**), but it is interesting to observe that both men and women in NCF hold more naive perceptions than women in CF (contrast with **Table 25**).

There are significant gender differences regarding the anticipation of future career/family conflicts and how they will be resolved. As **Table 37** indicates, women anticipate more conflicts and believe that to obtain their resolution they will have to give priority to their family over their career (47% women compared to 28% men). This priority given by women to family over career is a stable finding that can be found also among women in all fields of study combined (**Table 14**).

Table 36
Views of Gender Conditions in Country of Origin by Gender

View	Women	Men	T-test
Equality of gender in the labor market	2.15 (.63)	2.15 (.62)	.03
Equality of school attainment	3.33 (1.02)	3.43 (.97)	.68
Expectations of teachers toward men and women	2.39 (.90)	2.38 (.77)	−.05

Figures in parentheses are standard deviations.

Congruent with the priority of family over career, fewer women than men in nonconventional fields imagine themselves 15 years from now to be working fulltime, married, and with children (63% of the women compared to 87% of the men; chi-square = 16.35, p = .01). Gender differences regarding future family situations, in consequence, are strong and statistically significant. While most women see themselves married and with children, a number of them (14%) anticipate working only parttime. Significantly, an equal proportion of women (14%) see themselves married, working fulltime, but without children.

The majority of NCF men (57%), then, anticipate no career/family conflicts, congruent with our theory. More women than men, in contrast, anticipate that there will be conflicts and that conflicts will be resolved so that family matters will take precedence (**Table 37**). These findings are somewhat surprising, because we expected NCF women to be more assertive of their career rights. The findings are also discouraging, because they further confirm the profile of NCF women as being traditional in many aspects of social life. As suggested by the findings, NCF women — even more than CF women — subscribe to the dominant cultural view of women as primarily wives and mothers.

Table 37
Expectations Concerning Family and Career Conflict by Gender

	Women	Men
No conflict anticipated	36 (36)	39 (57)
There will be conflicts but family needs will take precedence	47 (47)	19 (28)
There will be conflicts but career needs will take precedence	17 (17)	11 (16)
	100 (100)	69 (101)

Chi-square = 7.86; d.f. = 2; statistically significant at the .02 level.
Figures in parentheses denote percentages.

Regarding strategies NCF students would follow if their spouse opposed their working outside the home, no gender differences occur. Most NCF men and women would opt for marriage and try to change their spouses' position before marriage. It is curious that although the possibility of a wife's opposing the husband's working outside the home is remote, the distribution of responses of men and women to this item is almost identical (**Table 38**).

Table 38
Options of Unmarried Students if Spouse Is Opposed
to Work After Marriage

Option	Women	Men
Choose marriage and forget career	3 (5)	1 (2)
Choose marriage and hope that spouse will change mind after marriage	5 (7)	3 (7)
Choose marriage and try to change future spouse's mind before marriage	34 (52)	25 (54)
Choose career and forget marriage	24 (36)	17 (37)
	66 (100)	46 (100)

Chi-square = .51, d.f. = 3, n.s.
Figures in parentheses denote percentages.

Additional evidence that NCF women are traditional individuals regarding family and domestic responsibilities is offered in **Table 39**.

Table 39
Degree of Support from Spouse for Future Career

Type of Support	Women	Men
Very supportive of my career; spouse will, if necessary, give priority to job demands regarding location, schedules, and travel	7 (18)	15 (47)
Very supportive of my career, but spouse's own career demands take priority	17 (44)	1 (3)
Very supportive of my career; all career moves between us have equal weight	15 (38)	13 (41)
Not very supportive of my career demands; sometimes this is a source of conflict at home	0	2 (6)
Not at all supportive of my career; sometimes this undermines my career	0	1 (3)
	39 (100)	32 (100)

Chi-square = 19.77; d.f. = 4; statistically significant at the .001 level.

Among those students who are married, strong gender differences emerge in the degree of support expected from their actual spouses. Many men (47%) expect that their spouses will be highly supportive of their future career, but few women expect similar support (18%). Remarkably, women in NCF expect less full support from their spouses than the overall pool of female married graduate students. **Table 16** indicates that 26% of women in the total sample of graduate women expect unconditional, top-priority support from their husbands, yet only 18% of NCF women expect this, even though they have invested much effort and sacrifice in their studies. The majority of NCF women do expect support (**Table 39**), but concede that their husbands' career will have priority over their own. Such an eventuality is foreseen by only 3% of the men.

Knowledge of Feminism and Feminism Scores

Knowledge of women's issues is lowest among students in NCF, particularly among NCF women. While NCF women attain a score of 2.25 in their self-reported understanding of gender issues, women in CF attain a score of 2.67 (see **Table 29**). It is clear then that NCF women are relatively unaware of important social issues. Women in NCF are very similar to NCF men in obtaining very little knowledge of women's issues through their regular courses. They are very similar also in not being exposed to women's studies and in not participating in feminist groups.

Table 40
Knowledge and Sources of Information About Gender Issues by Gender

	Women	Men	T-test
Knowledge of women's issues	2.25 (.71)	2.36 (.84)	.87
Source of Knowledge:			
Newspapers	3.40 (.57)	3.44 (.74)	.25
TV	3.09 (.84)	3.20 (.77)	.61
Women's courses at univ.	1.74 (1.01)	1.60 (.86)	−.58
General courses at univ.	1.59 (.73)	1.55 (.82)	−.23
Informal conversations	2.85 (.95)	2.56 (1.07)	−1.25
Participation in feminist groups	1.60 (.85)	1.60 (.90)	.15

Figures in parentheses are standard deviations.

Nonetheless, NCF women have a greater propensity toward feminist attitudes than NCF men. Seven of the eight items in the scale show significant differences by gender. The women score higher than men in six of the seven items; the anomalous exception is the more frequent assertion by NCF men than NCF women that a woman should be as free as a man to propose marriage.

Table 41

Total Scale and Item Means in Feminism Scale by Gender

Item	Women	Men	T-test
1. Because of past discrimination against women in many kinds of jobs, they should be given preference over equally-qualified men	2.16 (1.08)	1.81 (.95)	−2.23*
2. A woman should be as free as a man to propose marriage	3.06 (.98)	3.53 (.69)	3.80*
3. A woman should not expect to go to exactly the same places or to have quite the same freedom of action as a man	3.14 (.92)	3.03 (.93)	−1.10
4. In general, the father should have greater authority than the mother in bringing up the children	3.38 (.97)	3.02 (.97)	−2.52*
5. A married woman should not accept a job that requires her to be away from home overnight	2.89 (1.06)	2.09 (1.03)	−5.06*
6. Certain jobs should be done by women and certain jobs should be done by men	2.58 (1.09)	1.96 (.94)	−3.97*
7. Wife and husband should share the economic responsibility of supporting a family	3.55 (.69)	3.10 (7.66)	−4.15*
8. Women with small and school-age children should not work outside the home unless absolutely necessary	2.81 (1.03)	2.24 (.94)	−3.82*
Total Scale	23.69 (4.20)	20.78 (3.83)	−4.69*

* Statistically significant at the .05 level.

Summary

Teachers and professionals in the field are identified as strong influences in the selection of nonconventional fields by men and women, with parents having weaker roles. NCF women emerge as different from NCF men in that they are more utilitarian in their field of study choice. However, they tend to dislike the competitive nature of their field. The mothers of NCF women have an infrequent but influential role in the selection of field. NCF women prefer to have role models of their own sex, even though few female role models are available in their disciplines.

These women hold excessively rosy views about gender equality in their country of origin and at the same time readily endorse societal definitions of women as primarily wives and mothers. They score higher on feminist attitudes than their male counterparts, yet they reveal few progressive attitudes concerning their own decisions about family and marriage responsibilities. In all, women in nonconventional fields seem to arrive at these fields after protracted choices to which significant others express opposition. These NCF women seek and enter nonconventional fields by virtue of their skills in math and science, but they do not possess the gender consciousness that might forecast assertive and innovative roles as they assume professional positions. Indeed, NCF women exhibit a dismaying level of conformity with current gender relations in society.

IV.
Field of Study Choices Among Undergraduate Students

In this section, we examine the process of field of study selection at a younger age. Our purpose is twofold: to see whether the various forces that impinge upon field choices are stable over time and to detect whether certain actors and experiences have a greater influence on younger individuals.

As noted earlier, our sample of undergraduates was limited to juniors and seniors. Their distribution by level of study and gender was as follows:

Table 42
Undergraduate Student Distribution by Level of Study

	Women	Men
Junior	68 (35)	46 (43)
Senior	129 (65)	62 (57)
	197 (100)	108 (100)

Figures in parentheses denote percentages.

Differences Between Male and Female Undergraduate Students

Reasons for Selecting a Field of Study

As indicated earlier, we asked the respondents to identify as many reasons as applied in their field of study decision. The pattern of responses of the undergraduate students, in contrast to that of graduate students, shows no statistically significant differences by gender. The most commonly identified top reasons for selecting a field of study are the appeal of the discipline *per se* and the potential of that field for future employment.

It is interesting to observe that a sizable group of students state that a reason for selecting their fields was that it would not conflict with family responsibilities (16% for both men and women). Even in this response, contrary to theoretical expectations, there are no gender differences. A nontrivial number of students (10%) also said they were in their field because their families expected them to be. Compared with graduate students, the undergraduates reflect a greater sensitivity to parents and family responsibility (**Table 43**). It would seem, thus, that as individuals get older, they attribute more of their actions to their own volition and preference. But the undergraduate level data indicate that some of these influences may be internalized over time and then redefined as being one's own.

Table 43

Reasons for Field Selection by Gender in Absolute and Relative Numbers

Reason	Women	Men	Chi-square
1. Field will lead to definite employment opportunities	120 (59)	67 (60)	.03
2. It is a field that will not create conflict with future family responsibilities	32 (16)	18 (16)	.01
3. It is a field whose content interests me very much regardless of occupational potential	139 (69)	75 (68)	.01
4. The admission criteria for this field are not very rigorous	6 (3)	7 (6)	2.00
5. My family expects me to enter this field	20 (10)	11 (10)	.01

Figures in parentheses denote percentages. The N is greater than the sample due to multiple responses for this item.

Likes and Dislikes Regarding Selected Fields

Only two preferences distinguish men and women undergraduates in their selection of field. First, more men than women like their field because it requires math and science skills. Liking and disliking math seems to start quite early in the students' schooling experience, perhaps in high school or even before. Yet the salience of either math or verbal skills as the best liked features of a field is not as great as at the graduate level. Our graduate student data show (see **Table 6**) that what appears as the preference of only a few at the undergraduate level becomes intensified at the graduate level, particularly the preference for fields that require math/science skills. This increase in subject preference at the graduate level indicates that the undergraduate experience for women is different from that of men, and that this experience builds upon preferences and competencies students bring from high school (or earlier). It also indicates that the undergraduate experience does little to develop a taste for math and science courses among women. Likewise, it suggests that the undergraduate experience does little to modify conventional subject preferences of students.

The other statistically significant difference between men and women undergraduates is that more men than women like their fields because of their competitive atmosphere (**Table 45**).

As for the disliked features of their field, no gender differences emerge among the undergraduates, and their responses offer a pattern similar to that found at the graduate level.

Table 44
Likes and Dislikes in Selected Field of Study

Likes	Women	Men	Chi-square
The discipline is of great interest to me.	109 (54)	65 (59)	.81
The discipline requires math/science skills.	47 (23)	37 (33)	13.09**
The discipline requires verbal skills/English.	16 (8)	14 (13)	9.23*
The field offers many possibilities for finding a job.	68 (34)	40 (36)	.53
The field has a high prestige.	27 (14)	23 (21)	3.24
I like its competitive atmosphere.	21 (10)	22 (20)	8.44*
The field is not dominated by one sex.	16 (8)	13 (12)	5.51
Dislikes			
The coursework is very difficult.	58 (29)	28 (25)	.80
The field offers few possibilities for finding a job.	16 (8)	8 (7)	4.29
The field requires math/science skills.	6 (3)	6 (5)	4.99
The field requires verbal skills/English.	22 (11)	8 (7)	5.06
The field has low prestige.	7 (4)	6 (5)	2.62
I dislike its competitive atmosphere.	25 (12)	19 (17)	3.57
The field is dominated by one sex.	27 (13)	2 (11)	3.93
There is nothing I dislike about my field.	73 (36)	40 (36)	4.66

 * Statistically significant at the .10 level.
** Statistically significant at the .05 level.
   Figures in parentheses denote percentages.

The Role of Significant Others

In the comparison between men and women undergraduates, no statistically significant differences emerge in the influence of significant others upon field selection. The father, mother, and professionals in the selected field are identified as the most influential. By contrast, graduate students identified teachers and professionals in the selected field as the most influential. Comparing the mean levels of influence of significant others upon field choices made by undergraduate and graduate students (**Tables 21 and 45**), it is clear that undergraduates are much more susceptible to the influence of others, particularly that of parents.

Table 45
Mean Level of Influence of Significant Others by Gender

Significant Other	Women	Men	T-test
Father	2.79 (1.04)	2.75 (1.08)	− .27
Mother	2.70 (1.01)	2.51 (1.07)	− 1.45
Teacher/s	2.33 (1.00)	2.25 (1.05)	− .68
School counselor	1.83 (.88)	2.06 (1.03)	1.94
Professionals in the field	2.71 (1.04)	2.77 (1.15)	.66
College peers	2.32 (1.01)	2.30 (1.00)	− .18
Relatives/siblings	2.19 (1.00)	2.14 (1.03)	− .40
Mass media	2.26 (1.00)	2.25 (1.00)	− .16

Figures in parentheses are standard deviations.

Undergraduates report also having received messages to dissuade them from their current field of study. These messages were reported by 71% of men and 61% of women. In response to an open-ended question, asking the reasons for such dissuasion, the responses listed in **Table 46** emerge. The most frequently cited reason for leaving a field is related to unpromising work opportunities in the profession. This reason accounts for 31% of the women's responses and for 33% of the men's responses.

For women, however, the next most frequent reasons dissuading them from their current fields are gender-related. These reasons account for 26% in the case of women but for only 7% in the case of men. It is interesting to observe that a good number of the messages (13%) intended to dissuade women from their fields concern the field being "for men."

Clearly gender *per se* is offered as a reason for not entering certain fields. In addition, there are a number of reasons that may be indirectly gender-related, such as the lack of need for further study or the risk of becoming hurt in a given occupation. Those reasons are reported by 10% of women in contrast with 3% of men.

Table 46
Reasons for Dissuading Undergraduate Students from Current Field of Study by Gender

Reasons	Women		Men	
Gender-related reasons				
It is a field for men	9	(13)	0	
Girls cannot do it	2	(3)	0	
Will take the individual far away from home	4	(6)	2	(7)
Will offer difficulties for marriage and family	2	(3)	0	
Scholarship withdrawn when sponsors learned recipient was a woman	1	(1)	0	
Subtotal	18	(26)	2	(7)
Possibly gender-related reasons				
Religious reasons	1	(1)	0	
Student is too old	3	(4)	0	
No need for further studies	3	(4)	1	(3)
Can be injured in that profession	1	(1)	0	
Subtotal	7	(10)	1	(3)
Job-related				
Will command low salary	6	(9)	5	(17)
Not a marketable field. No jobs/difficult to find jobs in that field	13	(19)	4	(13)
Too competitive atmosphere	3	(4)	1	(3)
Subtotal	22	(32)	10	(33)
Academic reasons				
Not a sufficiently good student	3	(4)	3	(10)
The field is too difficult	9	(13)	5	(17)
No status in profession	4	(6)	4	(13)
Studies in field are too expensive	2	(3)	2	(7)
Changing fields is not advisable	1	(1)	1	(3)
Too ideological/political field	2	(3)	0	
Subtotal	21	(29)	15	(50)
U.S. a poor influence; student might not return	0		2	(7)
Student too extroverted for field	1	(1)	0	
Total	69	(100)	30	(100)

Figures in parentheses denote percentages.

A common set of reasons for dissuading men from their selected fields are academic reasons (reported by 50%); for women, academic reasons are less frequently mentioned (29%). Men do receive messages that could be interpreted as being gender-oriented in nature, but these are much fewer in number than those directed toward women. Job-related reasons seem to affect male and female undergraduates similarly.

As was the case for graduate-level women, the distribution of responses among undergraduates indicates that a large number of the messages received by women are due to social definitions of what are appropriate feminine fields of study and work. On the basis of our questionnaire data, we cannot demonstrate that negative gender-related messages were successful in deterring some women from their first choice of field, but given the high proportion of this type of message, it is clear that gender-related messages are very much part of the process of socialization and that, hence, they must function as important elements in the choice of field decisions.

The Presence of Role Models

The undergraduates tend to select role models after field selection. No gender differences emerge on this variable. In both cases, almost half of the group reports having a role model.

Table 47
Presence and Time of Identification of Role Models by Gender

| | Women | | Men | | Chi- |
	Yes	No	Yes	No	square
Reports an adult whom student considers an example to follow	95 (48)	105 (52)	60 (54)	51 (46)	.97
Role model prior to choice of field	45 (43)	59 (57)	25 (40)	38 (60)	.08

Confirming a tendency observed at the graduate level, undergraduate students tend to choose role models of their own gender (**Table 48**). And it seems that the younger the students, the greater their identification with persons of their own sex; in other words, more undergraduates than graduate students were found to have like-sex models. A possible explanation for the sizable decrease of female models at the graduate level is that female professors are fewer in number at that level.

Table 48
Gender of Role Model by Gender of the Undergraduate Student

	Women	Men
Female role model	51 (54)	2 (3)
Male role model	44 (46)	58 (97)
	95 (100)	60 (100)

Chi-square = 41.43; d.f. = 1; statistically significant at the .001 level.
Figures in parentheses represent percentages.

Views of Gender in Society

Overall, undergraduates believe that their national societies are egalitarian with regard to gender opportunities in the labor force and the educational system. It is likely that this positive view is related to the relatively sheltered and comfortable life of the undergraduate students in their home country. In fact, only 34% of the women and 33% of the men report having worked before. While no gender differences emerge on two of three indicators, women tend to have a more positive (i.e., naive) view than men concerning one indicator: the situation of women in the labor force (**Table 49**).

Table 49
Views of Gender Conditions in Country of Origin by Gender

View	Women	Men	T-test
Equality of gender in the labor market	2.57 (1.00)	2.07 (1.04)	−4.16**
Equality of school attainment	3.43 (.96)	3.45 (.91)	.22
Expectations of teachers toward men and women	2.53 (.61)	2.59 (.67)	.75

* Statistically significant at the .05 level.
Figures in parentheses are standard deviations.

With regard to future career and family decisions, strong differences emerge between men and women undergraduates. Clearly, women anticipate more conflicts than men. Moreover, a large number of women expect that when dilemmas do emerge between family and career choices, family needs will take precedence. The proportion of undergraduate women reporting this expectation (57%) is larger than that of graduate women (46%). This finding suggests one of two alternative processes is at work: either the more recent generations of women are becoming more accepting of traditional patriarchal ideologies; or, conversely, graduate-level women, who have invested greater time and effort in a field of study may be less willing to accept family over career priorities.

Table 50
Expectations Concerning Family and Career Conflict by Gender

	Women	Men
No conflict anticipated	63 (32)	62 (58)
There will be conflicts but family needs will take precedence	111 (57)	30 (28)
There will be conflicts but career needs will take precedence	21 (10)	15 (14)

Chi-square = 24.51; d.f. 3; statistically significant at the .001 level.
Figures in parentheses denote percentages.

Strong gender differences also emerge between male and female undergraduates concerning their options should their future spouses oppose their working outside the home. Marriage is the preferred option for everybody; however, many fewer women than men (19% versus 30%) would choose a career at the expense of marriage. Also, more women than men would try to obtain their spouse's support for working before they marry. The women's belief that it is easy to change the spouse's position is intriguing. It reveals either a significant ability on their part to negotiate the terms of a future marriage contract or dubious confidence in being able to persuade future husbands to be supportive of their careers.

Table 51
Options of Unmarried Students if Spouse Is Opposed
to Work After Marriage

Option	Women	Men
Choose marriage and forget career	10 (5)	2 (2)
Choose marriage and hope that spouse will change mind after marriage	23 (12)	20 (19)
Choose marriage and try to change future spouse's mind before marriage	125 (64)	52 (50)
Choose career and forget marriage	37 (19)	31 (30)

Chi-square = 10.08; d.f. = 3; statistically significant at the .02 level.
Figures in parentheses denote percentages.

On the positive side, there is an extremely low proportion of women who would prefer marriage without a career (5%) and a relatively higher percentage (19%) who would prefer a career without marriage. These findings contrast strongly with comparable data of U.S. freshmen and senior girls obtained a decade ago. Komarovsky (1979) found that 5% of the U.S. women preferred not to work after marriage but only 2% wanted a career without marriage. It can be seen that today women from other countries envisage working after marriage, and that many more than in the past would contemplate a professional career without getting married.

Knowledge of Feminism and Feminism Score

Curiously, undergraduate men report greater levels of knowledge about gender issues than do undergraduate women. While the mean for both groups is low, between "somewhat knowledgeable" and "not very knowledgeable," there is a statistically significant difference between men and women.

Among those who consider themselves very or somewhat knowledgeable, important gender differences exist in the sources of their knowledge. More women identify as useful sources their participation in general courses at the university, participation in specific women's courses, and involvement in feminist groups.

It is unclear why men are less likely than women to consider general courses at the university as important sources of gender knowledge. One reason may be that men tend to take more courses in science and math, courses that generally do not treat gender issues.

As in the case of graduate students, newspapers and TV are more important sources of information on gender issues for undergraduates than formal coursework at the university. Even though more undergraduate women than men take women's studies and participate in feminist groups, they still rate the mass media as more important than their specific feminist involvement in developing and maintaining their awareness of gender issues.

Table 52

Knowledge and Sources of Information About Gender Issues by Gender

	Women	Men	T-test
Knowledge of women's issues	2.32 (.77)	2.54 (.81)	2.29**
Source of Knowledge:			
Newspapers	3.28 (.79)	3.40 (.71)	.96
TV	3.13 (.91)	3.22 (.87)	.64
General courses at univ.	2.37 (.96)	1.96 (.94)	−2.61**
Women's courses at univ.	2.43 (1.07)	1.90 (1.13)	−2.70**
Informal conversations	2.70 (.99)	2.62 (1.12)	−.50
Participation in feminist groups	2.09 (1.01)	1.55 (.85)	−3.28**

** Statistically significant at the .05 level or below.
Figures in parentheses are standard deviations.

Our scale of feminist attitudes reveals significant gender differences on all eight items as well as on the overall scale; except on one item, women score higher. The one item concerns the belief that "a woman should be as free as a man to propose marriage." Consistently, more men than women endorse this belief. This is an intriguing result. On the one hand, it reflects women's strong adherence to a patriarchal norm closely linked with a key institution in society — the norm that women should be passive regarding marriage. On the other hand, it may indicate that men feel oppressed by having to take all the initiative about marriage. Perhaps men feel that good possibilities are lost because women are only passive actors?

Table 53

Total Scale and Item Means in Feminism Scale by Gender

Item	Women	Men	T-test
1. Because of past discrimination against women in many kinds of jobs, they should be given preference over equally qualified men	2.45 (1.07)	2.03 (1.00)	−3.31**
2. A woman should be as free as a man to propose marriage	2.90 (.98)	3.35 (.84)	4.35**
3. A woman should not expect to go to exactly the same places or to have quite the same freedom of action as a man	3.25 (.94)	2.82 (1.07)	−3.66**
4. In general, the father should have greater authority than the mother in bringing up the children	3.32 (.97)	2.95 (1.17)	−3.00**
5. A married woman should not accept a job that requires her to be away from home overnight	2.57 (1.00)	2.07 (1.04)	−4.16**
6. Certain jobs should be done by women and certain jobs should be done by men	2.45 (1.14)	2.01 (1.10)	−2.77**
7. Wife and husband should share the economic responsibility of supporting a family	3.48 (.72)	3.18 (.91)	−3.16**
8. Women with small and school-age children should not work outside the home unless absolutely necessary	2.50 (1.21)	2.04 (.97)	−3.89**
Total Scale	22.97 (4.06)	20.50 (4.48)	−4.80**

** Statistically significant at the .05 level or below.

Summary

In the comparison between men and women at the undergraduate level, few significant differences emerge in the factors shaping their field of study choices. While these differences are few in number, they are nonetheless critical. Men tend to choose fields because they require math and science skills; among women, there is a preference for fields that involve verbal skills and English. Many more women than men undergraduates report a role model of their own sex, even though this person emerges usually only after field selection. The undergraduate women express a much greater willingness than men to allow family needs to dominate career needs; they also see marriage as more important than work and feel confident they can make their future husbands support their career. The women's choice of family over career possibly leads them to career choices that are compatible with family life in terms of requirements of time and location. Because of this domestic perspective, women may eliminate a number of fields as "inappropriate."

When confronted with a concrete and personal situation, undergraduate women assume the traditional roles of women. However, when asked to express their feminist attitudes in more abstract, impersonal terms, undergraduate women clearly show more progressive gender attitudes than men. This finding supports previous social science research demonstrating that general values may be more egalitarian than our actual behaviors. In subsequent sections, we will explore how those general values associated with feminism affect field of study choices.

Undergraduate Women in Nonconventional and Conventional Fields

How are those women who move into nonconventional fields different from those in conventional fields?

Reasons for Selecting a Field of Study

Four statistically significant differences emerge in the reasons for field selection identified by NCF and CF undergraduate women. These concern, primarily, the employment potential of the selected discipline. NCF women persistently choose occupations because of their utilitarian value: 75% of NCF undergraduate women indicate this reason, contrasted with 37% of CF women.

Table 54

Reasons for Field Selection by NCF and CF Women in Absolute and Relative Numbers

Reason	NCF Women	CF Women	Chi-square
1. Field will lead to definite employment opportunities	85 (75)	7 (37)	12.89**
2. It is a field that will not create conflict with future family responsibilities	15 (13)	5 (25)	1.82
3. It is a field whose content interests me very much regardless of occupational potential	64 (57)	17 (85)	5.74*
4. The admission criteria for this field are not very rigorous	0	3 (15)	17.34**
5. My family expects me to enter this field	16 (14)	0	3.21*
6. Government or funding agency promoted the field	18 (16)	1 (5)	1.65

  * Statistically significant at the .10 level.
 ** Statistically significant at the .05 level or below.
    Figures in parentheses denote percentages. The N is greater than the sample due to multiple responses for this item.

Other differences include an interest in the discipline *per se*, which appeals, perhaps surprisingly, mostly to CF women, and a preference for not very rigorous admission criteria for the selected fields (not a surprising finding, particularly if we realize more CF than NCF women enter fields because they do not like math and science and, quite likely, do not perform well in these subjects either; math, as we know, is frequently an important subject in admission exams). A second unexpected finding is that several NCF but no CF women report entering into a field because of family expectations. This indicates that families play both supportive and nonsupportive roles in NCF selection. The factors that lead parents to be supportive of daughters' NCF choices are explained in a later chapter when we discuss a causal analytical model.

Likes and Dislikes Regarding Selected Fields

The features female students in NCF and CF like and dislike most in their selected fields, as discussed earlier, were explored by asking students to rank the three features they liked best and least about their fields. **Table 55** concentrates on only those responses which were identified as most liked and least liked features.

Table 55

Likes and Dislikes of NCF and CF Women in Their Selected Field of Study

Likes	NCF Women	CF Women	Chi-square
The discipline is of great interest to me	46 (41)	17 (85)	13.81**
The discipline requires math/science skills	35 (31)	1 (5)	16.47**
The discipline requires verbal skills/ English	6 (5)	2 (10)	9.75**
The field offers many possibilities for finding a job	51 (45)	4 (20)	11.62**
The field has a high prestige	18 (16)	1 (5)	9.51**
I like its competitive atmosphere	12 (11)	1 (5)	.86
The field is not dominated by one sex	9 (8)	3 (15)	5.36
Dislikes			
The coursework is very difficult	39 (35)	1 (5)	7.69*
The field offers few possibilities for finding a job	3 (3)	4 (20)	12.69**
The field requires math/science skills	5 (4)	0	1.30
The field requires verbal skills/English	16 (14)	0	5.71
The field has low prestige	2 (2)	3 (15)	11.22**
I dislike its competitive atmosphere	17 (15)	2 (10)	3.98**
The field is dominated by one sex	15 (13)	0	5.24
There is nothing I dislike about my field	35 (31)	11 (55)	5.07

  * Statistically significant at the .10 level.
 ** Statistically significant at the .05 level or below.
    Figures in parentheses denote percentages.

The most liked features of the students' field correspond to the reasons given for selecting it. NCF women like fields for their math and science content, and for leading to a job; CF women, in contrast, like fields that involve verbal skills. NCF women also like their fields for having high prestige. On this item, undergraduate women show a reversal vis-a-vis graduate-level women, as a larger number of CF graduate-level women identify as one of the most liked features of their field its having high prestige. We are unsure of how to explain this contradiction.

The Role of Significant Others in Field Selection

As for significant others, parents emerge as the most influential actors for both NCF and CF women, but no statistically significant differences exist between the two groups. Significant differences do emerge in the influence of teachers and counselors. Teachers are found to play a traditional role, as they are identified as influential in shaping mostly conventional choices. School counselors are identified as having the weakest impact on field choices; nonetheless, they play a more progressive role than teachers, since they encourage more NCF than CF women.

Table 56

Mean Level of Influence of Significant Others Among NCF and CF Women

Significant Other	NCF Women	CF Women	T-test
Father	2.81 (1.01)	2.63 (.95)	−.73
Mother	2.70 (1.00)	2.47 (.90)	−.95
Teacher/s	2.28 (1.00)	2.75 (1.00)	1.69*
School counselor	1.89 (.92)	1.42 (.64)	−1.80*
Professionals in the field	2.69 (1.05)	2.94 (.93)	.95
College peers	2.40 (1.03)	2.26 (1.10)	−.46
Relatives/siblings	2.32 (.99)	2.11 (.85)	−.81
Mass media	2.33 (.99)	2.46 (1.06)	.49

* Statistically significant at the .10 level.
Figures in parentheses are standard deviations.

The Presence of Role Models

Significantly fewer undergraduate NCF women report a role model compared to CF women. This pattern was also detected among NCF graduate-level women but it failed to attain statistical significance. Why do NCF women report fewer role models? One possible and perhaps obvious interpretation is that they are exposed to few individuals they can identify with.

No differences emerge between NCF and CF in their selection of role models prior to the selection of field. Unlike graduate women, more undergraduate women report having had a role model prior to the selection of field.

This greater identification of a role model as influential prior to the selection of a field at the undergraduate level may reflect the greater importance of significant others and role models at earlier stages of intellectual and personal development. This finding indicates that we, as individuals, are susceptible to the actions and messages of others in earlier phases of our lives even though we tend to deny or minimize these influences as we grow older.

Table 57
Presence and Time of Identification of Role Models Among NCF and CF Women

	NCF Women		CF Women		Chi-square
	Yes	No	Yes	No	
Reports an adult whom student considers an example to follow	45 (40)	67 (60)	13 (65)	7 (35)	3.29*
Role model prior to choice of field	33 (65)	19 (37)	7 (50)	7 (50)	.83

* Statistically significant at the .05 level; d.f. = 1.

When asked to report the gender of their role models, CF women identify female role models to a much greater extent than NCF women. This difference is statistically significant. NCF women may well be selecting more male role models, because there are more male professionals and college professors in their field, although women, overall, prefer to have role models of their own sex. In fact, when NCF undergraduate women are compared to NCF graduate women, more undergraduates report having a female model (40% vs. 28%, respectively), very likely because more women professors are available at undergraduate levels.

Table 58
Gender of Role Model by NCF and CF Women

	NCF Women	CF Women
Female role model	19 (40)	9 (75)
Male role model	28 (60)	3 (25)
	47 (100)	12 (100)

Chi-square = 3.30; d.f. = 1; statistically significant at the .06 level.
Figures in parentheses represent percentages.

Views of Gender in Society

In a pattern also detected among graduate students, undergraduate NCF women hold more naive or unrealistic views of gender in society than CF students. These differences, as was the case for the graduate students, are weak and only one of them attains statistical significance, namely the belief about women's equality in the labor market, with NCF women holding a more optimistic view of equality than CF women.

Table 59
Views of Gender Conditions in Country of Origin by NCF and CF Women

View	NCF Women	CF Women	T-test
Equality of gender in the labor market	2.25 (.69)	1.85 (.87)	−2.29**
Equality of school attainment	3.54 (.81)	3.31 (1.00)	−1.09
Expectations of teachers toward men and women	2.57 (.58)	2.44 (.61)	−.88

** Statistically significant at the .05 level.
Figures in parentheses are standard deviations.

The same tendency observed before in NCF women graduate students concerning conflicts between career and family emerges also among NCF women undergraduates. The majority of these NCF undergraduates expect that family needs will take priority over their own career needs though there are no statistically significant differences between NCF and CF women. It is clear that the impact due to gender identity is greater than the impact produced by affiliation with a nonconventional field. Women may be in nontraditional fields but their obedience to established gender roles renders them very traditional in other aspects of social life.

Table 60
Expectations Concerning Family and Career Conflict
Among NCF and CF Women

	NCF Women	CF Women
No conflict anticipated	30 (27)	7 (35)
There will be conflicts but family needs will take precedence	73 (65)	10 (50)
There will be conflicts but career needs will take precedence	10 (9)	3 (15)

Chi-square = 1.67; d.f. = 2; non-statistically significant.
Figures in parentheses denote percentages.

Exploring attitudes with reference to a concrete case, undergraduates were asked for specific options in case of spouses' opposition to work after marriage. Most women, whether NCF or CF, would choose marriage. The majority, in either group, would try to change the spouse's mind before marriage. No statistically significant differences emerge in the comparison of NCF and CF women as to these options.

66

Table 61
Options of Unmarried Students if Spouse Is Opposed to Work After Marriage

Option	NCF Women	CF Women
Choose marriage and forget career	6 (5)	1 (5)
Choose marriage and hope that spouse will change mind after marriage	16 (14)	2 (11)
Choose marriage and try to change future spouse's mind before marriage	68 (61)	11 (58)
Choose career and forget marriage	21 (19)	5 (26)

Chi-square = .651; d.f. = 3; n.s.
Figures in parentheses denote percentages.

Knowledge of Feminism and Feminism Score

Table 62 shows that CF undergraduate women consider themselves more knowledgeable than NCF women regarding women's issues. This difference does not reach statistical significance, as is the case for graduate-level women. This finding suggests that the undergraduate experience of NCF women does not permit growth in sociopolitical dimensions beyond the confines of the scientific and technical fields. As time goes on, they have less general knowledge and more specialized knowledge. Thus, when women in nonconventional fields reach the graduate level, their knowledge of gender issues is still the same as that of undergraduates (2.25 and 2.29, respectively), while the gender knowledge of graduate women in conventional fields has increased to 2.67, from 2.44 at the undergraduate level.

Between these two groups of undergraduates, only two major differences emerge: NCF women report that TV is an important source of knowledge for them; CF women think that participation in feminist groups is an important source of knowledge about gender issues.

Table 62
Knowledge and Sources of Information About Gender Issues Among NCF and CF Women

	NCF Women	CF Women	T-test
Knowledge of women's issues	2.29 (.72)	2.44 (.92)	.77
Source of Knowledge:			
Newspapers	3.23 (.81)	3.25 (1.05)	.05
TV	3.36 (.82)	2.58 (1.16)	−2.75**
General courses at univ.	2.16 (.94)	2.63 (1.02)	1.48
Women's courses at univ.	2.69 (1.04)	2.75 (1.05)	1.34
Informal conversations	2.63 (1.07)	2.92 (.86)	.88
Participation in feminist groups	2.00 (.96)	2.72 (1.34)	2.07**

** Statistically significant at the .05 level or below.
Figures in parentheses are standard deviations.

Overall, CF undergraduates emerge as being more attuned to gender issues. They indicate greater exposure to multiple sources of knowledge, ranging from participation in feminist groups to involvement in informal conversations. The only exception, discussed above, is that more NCF than CF undergraduate women rate TV as an important source of knowledge. It is likely that NCF undergraduate women spend most of their time concentrating on their academic work and that, under these circumstances, TV becomes both a means of relaxation and the main source of non-academic information.

When compared on the feminist scale, NCF and CF undergraduate women show many common attitudes. The pattern of responses is remarkably similar also to that of the graduate women, with a tendency among CF undergraduate women to hold more progressive ideas than their NCF counterparts. Thus, CF undergraduate women score slightly higher than NCF women on 5 of the 8 scale items. This finding further corroborates our characterization of NCF undergraduate women as leading isolated, field-focused lives, and developing limited awareness and understanding of how gender operates in society.

Table 63
Total Scale and Item Means in Feminism Scale of NCF and CF Women

Item	NCF Women	CF Women	T-test
1. Because of past discrimination against women in many kinds of jobs, they should be given preference over equally qualified men	2.57 (1.09)	2.15 (1.08)	.19
2. A woman should be as free as a man to propose marriage	2.88 (.96)	2.90 (1.25)	.06
3. A woman should not expect to go to exactly the same place or to have quite the same freedom of action as a man	3.16 (.98)	3.30 (.97)	.55
4. In general, the father should have greater authority than the mother in bringing up the children	3.34 (.85)	3.60 (.88)	1.21
5. A married woman should not accept a job that requires her to be away from home overnight	2.44 (.93)	2.65 (1.08)	.89
6. Certain jobs should be done by women and certain jobs should be done by men	2.28 (1.12)	2.55 (1.14)	.98
7. Wife and husband should share the economic responsibility of supporting a family	3.50 (.68)	3.45 (.75)	−.32
8. Women with small and school-age children should not work outside the home unless absolutely necessary	2.49 (1.01)	2.30 (1.03)	−.79
Total Scale	22.71 (3.72)	22.90 (4.90)	1.74

** Statistically significant at the .05 level.

Summary

The profile of NCF contrasted to CF undergraduate women describes the former as persons who select a field with highly utilitarian purposes in mind, i.e., they expect to obtain a good job after completion of their studies. The NCF women like the fact that their fields require math and science skills.

Parents emerge as influential for undergraduate women in general, but no differences emerge in their influencing daughters to choose NCF or CF studies. Significant others that influence the choice of type of field are teachers and counselors, with the former influencing mainly conventional choices and the latter having a role, albeit a weak one, in influencing nonconventional choices.

The NCF women, as a group, do not hold particularly progressive views of gender in society. They are more naive than their CF counterparts and demonstrate a greater tendency to accept family needs over career needs. Their CF counterparts hold more progressive feminist ideas but the differences do not always reach statistical significance.

Women and Men in Nonconventional Fields

Reasons for Selecting a Field of Study

No real differences emerge in the comparison between men and women in nonconventional fields. Both women and men in nonconventional fields selected their fields mainly because of the employment potential the field has and because they are also extremely interested in the discipline *per se*. Essentially, then, women — no less than men — enter nonconventional fields for utilitarian reasons and because of concomitant personal predilections.

Table 64

Reasons for Field Selection by Gender in Absolute and Relative Numbers

Reason	Women	Men	Chi-square
1. Field will lead to definite employment opportunities	85 (75)	61 (68)	1.03
2. It is a field that will not create conflict with future family responsibilities	15 (13)	18 (20)	1.20
3. It is a field whose content interests me very much regardless of occupational potential	64 (57)	60 (67)	1.71
4. The admission criteria for this field are not very rigorous	0	4 (5)	3.08*
5. My family expects me to enter this field	16 (14)	11 (12)	.03

* Statistically significant at 0.5 level.
  Figures in parentheses denote percentages. The N is greater than the sample due to multiple responses for this item.

It is interesting to observe that many more NCF undergraduate women than undergraduate men make their field of study choices after being in the United States (50% of the women vs. 38% of the men; chi-square = 2.75, p = .09). This finding is of great importance, because it indicates that U.S. culture and the university environment lead as many as 50% of the international women students to consider undergraduate fields that they might not have entered otherwise.

Likes and Dislikes Regarding Selected Fields

Very few differences exist between men and women with respect to likes and dislikes regarding selected fields. The only significant difference in terms of likes concerns the interest in the discipline *per se*, which appeals more to men than to women. In terms of dislikes, more women than men in NCF dislike the fact that their fields require (some) verbal skills and English.

Table 65
Likes and Dislikes in Selected Field of Study

Likes	Women	Men	Chi-square
The discipline is of great interest to me	46 (41)	53 (59)	6.65*
The discipline requires math/science skills	35 (31)	33 (37)	5.52
The discipline requires verbal skills/ English	6 (5)	9 (10)	7.80*
The field offers many possibilities for finding a job	51 (45)	35 (39)	2.40
The field has a high prestige	18 (16)	18 (20)	1.52
I like its competitive atmosphere	12 (11)	19 (21)	5.60
The field is not dominated by one sex	9 (8)	8 (9)	3.90
Dislikes			
The coursework is very difficult	39 (35)	21 (23)	4.20
The field offers few possibilities for finding a job	3 (3)	4 (4)	1.79
The field requires math/science skills	5 (4)	2 (2)	3.36
The field requires verbal skills/ English	16 (14)	7 (8)	6.99**
The field has low prestige	2 (2)	6 (7)	3.83
I dislike its competitive atmosphere	17 (15)	17 (19)	4.87
The field is dominated by one sex	15 (13)	12 (13)	3.93
There is nothing I dislike about my field	35 (31)	33 (37)	2.19

 * Statistically significant at the .10 level.
 ** Statistically significant at the .05 level.
   Figures in parentheses denote percentages.

The Role of Significant Others in Field Selection

When comparing women and men in NCF, the role of significant others does not show a differential impact that is statistically significant. The most influential others continue to appear in the same order of importance as in previous analyses focusing on individuals in nonconventional fields. The father and mother appear as very influential, followed by professionals in the selected field.

According to the data, the mass media have a slightly stronger impact on influencing nonconventional choices than do school personnel such as teachers and counselors, a surprising finding in light of the career guidance functions the latter are supposed to play.

College peers are identified as more important than teachers by NCF women, which we take as additional corroboration of the importance of informal networks for women.

Table 66
Mean Level of Influence of Significant Others by Gender

Significant Other	Women	Men	T-test
Father	2.81 (1.01)	2.85 (1.07)	.29
Mother	2.70 (1.00)	2.52 (1.00)	−1.20
Teacher/s	2.28 (1.02)	2.19 (1.01)	−.57
School counselor	1.89 (1.01)	2.01 (.92)	.84
Professionals in the field	2.69 (1.05)	2.73 (1.18)	.29
College peers	2.40 (1.03)	2.30 (1.01)	−.62
Relatives/siblings	2.32 (.99)	2.15 (1.09)	−1.11
Mass media	2.33 (.99)	2.28 (1.00)	−.27

Figures in parentheses are standard deviations.

The Presence of Role Models

Fewer undergraduate women than men in nonconventional fields report a role model, and there are statistically significant differences between the two groups. This pattern — of fewer role models — is stronger than at the graduate level and is somewhat difficult to interpret. Does it mean that undergraduate women lead a more isolated existence than female graduate students? We would have expected more individuals available as role models at the undergraduate than at the graduate level.

Undergraduates in NCF report having a role model selected before their field selection; although these percentages appear sizable, they fail to reach statistical significance.

Table 67

Presence and Time of Identification of Role Models by Gender

| | Women | | Men | | Chi- |
	Yes	No	Yes	No	square
Reports an adult whom student considers an example to follow	45 (40)	67 (60)	49 (54)	41 (46)	3.52*
Role model prior to choice of field	33 (64)	19 (36)	29 (58)	21 (42)	.13

* Statistically significant at the .05 level.

According to **Table 67**, male and female undergraduates in NCF show different patterns in the selection of role models. All men report having only male role models, while a large percentage of the women (40%) report having a female role model. Considering that students in nonconventional fields are exposed to more male than female figures (professors, authors of books, successful professionals, etc.), it is patently clear that women students make a deliberate attempt to acquire role models of the same sex.

Table 68

Gender of Role Model by Gender of the Undergraduate Student

	Women	Men
Female role model	19 (40)	0
Male role model	28 (60)	49 (100)
	47 (100)	49 (100)

Chi-square = 22.21; d.f. = 1; statistically significant at the .001 level.
Figures in parentheses represent percentages.

Views of Gender in Society

As **Table 69** shows, NCF women have a greater tendency to be naive than NCF men about gender conditions in their home country; these differences are slight and only one of them reaches statistical significance: NCF women are more likely to believe that the labor market presents few inequalities along sex lines.

Table 69

Views of Gender Conditions in Country of Origin by Gender

View	Women	Men	T-test
Equality of gender in the labor market	2.25 (.69)	2.04 (.61)	−2.22**
Equality of school attainment	3.54 (.81)	3.46 (.90)	−.64
Expectations of teachers toward men and women	2.57 (.58)	2.60 (.67)	.25

** Statistically significant at the .05 level.
Figures in parentheses are standard deviations.

Comparing men and women in NCF with regard to expectations of conflict between family and career (**Table 70**), it is evident that the majority of men (60%) do not expect family needs to conflict with career needs. The majority of women, in contrast, do anticipate conflicts. Moreover, these women are prepared to let family demands take precedence over their own career needs. These views of the men and women undergraduates reveal their strong internalization of gender roles and relations in society. They also indicate that women in NCF are not likely to take on important "change agent" functions when they acquire positions of professional stature.

Table 70

Expectations Concerning Family and Career Conflict by Gender

Expectations	Women	Men
No conflict anticipated	30 (27)	53 (60)
There will be conflicts but family needs will take precedence	73 (65)	24 (27)
There will be conflicts but career needs will take precedence	10 (9)	11 (13)
	113 (100)	88 (100)

Chi-square = 28.50; d.f. = 2; statistically significant at the .001 level.
Figures in parentheses denote percentages.

Table 71 shows that marriage is the preferred option for undergraduate NCF men and women. Differences appear in the decisions women and men would take should their spouses object to their working after marriage. More men than women would leave spouses who block their careers. More women are optimistic that they may be able, before marriage, to change their spouses' objections to their entering the labor force.

Women are also more committed to marriage. Even among women in NCF, a group of very employment-oriented individuals, 5% would give up their career if it conflicted with their spouses' position regarding women's working outside the home after marriage.

Table 71

Options of Unmarried Students if Spouse Is Opposed to Work After Marriage

Option	Women	Men
Choose marriage and forget career	6 (5)	1 (1)
Choose marriage and hope that spouse will change mind after marriage	16 (14)	17 (19)
Choose marriage and try to change future spouse's mind before marriage	68 (61)	44 (50)
Choose career and forget marriage	21 (19)	26 (30)
	(100)	(100)

Chi-square = 6.70; d.f. = 3; statistically significant at the .08 level.
Figures in parentheses denote percentages.

Knowledge of Feminism and Feminism Score

As in the case of the graduate students, undergraduate women in NCF know little about gender issues. In fact, they indicate less knowledge than their male counterparts. This analysis produces a statistically significant difference.

Among those who do know something about gender issues, women more often report exposure to general and specific women's courses at the university and participation in feminist groups than men. These findings have positive and negative implications. On the negative side, it is worrisome to see that NCF women, by their own admission, know less than NCF men regarding women's issues. On the other hand, it appears that a minority of NCF undergraduate women today are having greater exposure than NCF graduate-level women (compare with **Table 38**) to general and women's studies and extracurricular activities which are increasing their understanding of gender issues.

Table 72
Knowledge and Sources of Information About Gender Issues by Gender

	Women	Men	T-test
Knowledge of women's issues	2.29 (.72)	2.47 (.86)	1.61*
Source of Knowledge:			
Newspapers	3.23 (.81)	3.39 (.63)	1.09
TV	3.36 (.82)	3.24 (.82)	−.77
General courses at univ.	2.16 (.94)	1.77 (.85)	−2.08*
Women's courses at univ.	2.29 (1.04)	1.82 (1.21)	−2.04**
Informal conversations	2.63 (1.07)	2.64 (1.15)	−1.25
Participation in feminist groups	2.00 (.91)	1.46 (.74)	−2.87**

** Statistically significant at the .05 level or below.
   Figures in parentheses are standard deviations.

The feminist scale shows clear distinctions between NCF women and men. Consistently, women reveal a stronger sense of gender equality than men, and most of these differences are statistically significant at the .05 level or below. The only unexpected exception, noted throughout the performance of this scale, is the item stating that a woman should be able to propose marriage, which again receives more approval from men than women.

Table 73

Total Scale and Item Means in Feminism Scale by Gender

Item	Women	Men	T-test
1. Because of past discrimination against women in many kinds of jobs, they should be given preference over equally qualified men	2.57 (1.09)	2.04 (1.03)	−3.51**
2. A woman should be as free as a man to propose marriage	2.88 (.96)	3.37 (.84)	3.83**
3. A woman should not expect to go to exactly the same place or to have quite the same freedom of action as a man	3.16 (.98)	2.75 (1.03)	−2.93**
4. In general, the father should have greater authority than the mother in bringing up the children	3.34 (.85)	2.88 (1.12)	−3.29**
5. A married woman should not accept a job that requires her to be away from home overnight	2.44 (.93)	1.95 (.97)	−3.62**
6. Certain jobs should be done by women and certain jobs should be done by men	2.28 (1.07)	1.98 (1.07)	−1.89**
7. Wife and husband should share the economic responsibility of supporting a family	3.50 (.68)	3.12 (.92)	−3.39**
8. Women with small and school-age children should not work outside the home unless absolutely necessary	2.49 (1.01)	2.00 (.94)	−3.55**
Total Scale	22.71 (3.72)	20.13 (4.15)	−4.57**

** Statistically significant at the .05 level or below.

Summary

In the comparison of women and men undergraduates enrolled in NCF, there is a great deal of similarity in the reasons for selecting their field. For both groups, the employment opportunities afforded by the field is very important. Second in importance, also for both groups, is the individual's interest in the discipline *per se*, with women putting more weight on this preference than men.

Significant others are found to have similar levels of importance in influencing the selection of field, with parents and professionals in the field exerting the strongest influence. NCF women tend to endorse traditional societal norms regarding marriage and husband's dominance. They hold substantially more progressive views than NCF men regarding gender equality in society, but when asked to select among concrete options with regard to future life events, these women tend to be even more traditional than their male counterparts.

V.
A Causal Model
of Field
# of Study
Choices

We shall now carry out a multivariate analysis of the various factors influencing field of study choices among international students.[7]

---

[7]This more complex quantitative analysis explores cause-effect relationships using the soft-modeling technique known as the Latent Variable Path Analysis with Partial Least Squares Estimation (LVPLS for short). As Falk (1987) notes, this technique is based on numerous contributions from economics, political science, psychology, sociology, and statistics. Specifically, LPVLS is based on a mathematical framework developed by Wold (1980) and a software program designed by Lohmoeller (1984). Its use in the United States is incipient, although it is clear that it represents an important innovation in the use of quantitative methods in the social sciences.

The use of soft-modeling techniques permits social scientists to explore asymmetrical relationships without variables when their data fail to meet rigorous conditions required by statistical techniques such as maximum-likelihood estimation. LVPLS, by relying on least squares estimation, permits the use of data with the following characteristics:

Theoretical conditions:

1. Macro-level theories do not specify all salient-relevant variables.
2. The relationships between theoretical constructs and their manifestations are vague.
3. The relationships between constructs are uncertain but conjectural.

Our field-of-study choice model is based on a total of 11 variables, all previously discussed under our theoretical framework. These comprise 10 independent variables (family environment, prestige of field, individual's academic preparation, individual's academic performance, family influence, school agents' influence, views of gender in society, feminist attitudes, career commitment, and selection of field at the undergraduate level, and one dependent variable: selection of field at the graduate level). Some of these variables were examined in the previous comparative analysis. Others are investigated only in the causal model.

In the model that is discussed below, we treat our key variables as constructs or latent variables, assuming that their measurement can be only approximate. Each of these latent variables, in turn, is measured through a set of several manifest variables or indicators. When applied to graduate students, the model consists of all the variables identified above. When used on undergraduate data, the model drops the one variable that does not apply (the selection of field of study at the graduate level), and selection of field at the undergraduate level becomes the new dependent variable.

The theoretically-based model is applied first to all students at a given level (i.e., graduate or undergraduate). Then, it is applied only to women. Because of the low number of male cases, the use of the causal model with respect to men only is too unstable to produce meaningful results. Comparisons between men and women are then done indirectly, comparing coefficients for the general model (which comprises men and women) with those of the model applied to women only.

Definition and Operationalization of Variables

Family environment is defined by four indicators measuring mother's and father's level of education and the level of prestige of their occupation. The level of education of the parents was assessed through an 8-point item ranging from the incomplete primary to the Ph.D./M.D. level.

Measurement conditions:
4. Some or all of the manifest variables are categorical.
5. Manifest variables have some degree of unreliability.
6. Heteroscedasticity, or having residuals on manifest and latent variables correlated, exist.

Distributional conditions:
7. Distributions are nonnormal or unknown.

Practical conditions:
8. Cross-sectional, survey, secondary data, or quasi-experimental research designs are employed.
9. There are many manifest and latent variables.
10. Any number of cases are available.
11. Fast computer results are desirable. (Falk, 1987, pp. 6-7.)

In LVPLS, unlike conventional causal modeling approaches, a higher coefficient reflects a greater fit.

The other indicator of family environment, **parental occupational status**, is measured by a numerical scale used in the U.S. census and corrected to reflect also the presence of women in the occupations (Powers and Holmberg, 1982). Social scientists have worked on the measurement of occupational prestige across nations, and one such global scale has been developed by Treiman (1977). His work was not known to the researcher at the time of the scale selection; further, his scale does not reflect the gender adjustments made in the more recent work by Powers and Holmberg. Treiman's examination of occupational status throughout the world led him to the conclusion that, "the basic pattern is one of uniformity across regions in the degree of intercountry agreement in prestige evaluations; there is little real evidence of cultural differences in occupational prestige evaluations, at least as measured in this crude way" (p. 98). We will argue therefore that using a scale that reflects prestige criteria relevant to the United States is appropriate on two counts: the modern world is becoming increasingly more homogeneous, and individuals who come to study in this country most likely accept and will use U.S. definitions of occupational prestige. Notwithstanding differences regarding professions such as medicine, accounting, and teaching, considerable agreement exists in the status of professions, a category in which many of the students' parents are found.

The occupational prestige ratings utilized in the scale selected for our study include all occupations considered in the U.S. census, distinguish 12 different occupational categories and include all occupations considered in the U.S. census, rating them from 0 to 98 points. Although this scale has a category called "private household workers," we have added a thirteenth category to designate the occupation of many students' mothers. We call this category "homemakers" and assigned it a score of 25 points, which we consider to be a reasonable weight since housewives have much more prestige than housemaids.

Field prestige. This variable measures the extent to which the individuals considered the prestige of the field to be an important feature of the selected field of study. It was measured by a structured item that ranges from 0 (not important at all) to 3 points (extremely important).

Individual's academic performance. This variable assesses how students compared themselves with their peers in terms of their math and science performance while in high school. It is measured by a two-item scale in which each item consists of four points, ranging from considering oneself "below average" to being the "highest 1% of the class."

Individual's academic preparation. This is measured in terms of a four-item scale covering the number of years individuals studied mathematics, physics, chemistry, and calculus while in secondary school. This measure is based also on self-report.

Family influence on field selection. This construct is approximated through the use of three indicators: the degree to which the father, mother, and relatives were important influences in the selection of field made by the students. Their scoring ranges from 0 (not important at all) to 4 (very important).

Educational actors' influence on field selection. This measure also relies on three indicators: teachers, counselors, and professionals in the field. While the latter are not in schools, we have placed them in the same bloc as they represent an educational (albeit informal) influence. Their scoring also ranges from 0 to 4 along the same dimensions as in family influences.

Individual's view of gender in society. This is measured by a combined index probing the perception of three different areas of society and how women fare in them: (1) the occupational condition of women with regard to access to jobs in general; (2) the educational condition of women in terms of their achievement at all levels; and (3) the type of educational experience women undergo within the educational system in terms of treatment from teachers. The scores for each of these items range from 1 to 4. The ratings for this scale were recoded during the causal model testing, so that a greater perception of gender inequalities should influence the tendency to select a nonconventional field of study.

Feminism score. The feminism scale described earlier in this study (see p. 14) is divided into three indicators when utilized in the causal model. Items 4, 5, and 7 measure feminist attitudes regarding family relations; items 1, 6, and 8 cover work relations; and item 3 refers to social relations in general. (Item 2 was dropped, given the fact that it persistently worked in the opposite direction).

Career commitment. This variable is based on a combination of three items: the circumstances respondents envisage in the family; whether they anticipate becoming active professionals in their field; and the level of family support they anticipate from their husbands.

Conventionality of field of study. In the multivariate analysis, field of study is measured on an ordinal scale ranging from 0 to 4. The development of this scale was explained earlier, on p. 13).[8]

---

[8]As noted earlier, the independent variables in the model are based on one to four indicators. Our key concepts are considered as "latent" variables (given their elusive nature) and the indicators are posited to reflect an underlying dimension

The Graduate Students' Model

The results from testing the causal model (see **Figure B**) show that the family environment is a powerful factor in the selection of field of study. It does so by affecting directly the selection of undergraduate fields (.15) and, indirectly, the impact that the family will have in shaping field decisions (.31). But it should be noted that the impact of the family on field selection is not associated with selecting a nonconventional field. Students are influenced by parents, but this influence can be toward conventional or nonconventional fields.

Another mechanism by which the family environment affects field of study choice is by affecting the individual's perception of academic performance in math and science (.16). The wealthier the family environment, the stronger the individual's tendency to feel that she is a high academic performer. This perception, in turn, has a strong influence in the selection of nonconventional fields of study (.34).

The path coefficients in the model also reveal that the direct influences coming from the family do not have a substantial effect on the selection of the graduate field of study. The graduate students identify fathers and mothers as having influenced their field of study choices, yet a greater degree of influence on the part of these actors does not seem to result in a selection of nonconventional fields. An explanation for the lack of parental influence in the selection of nonconventional fields may be that when parents are influential on field choices, they provide advice for and against both conventional and nonconventional fields.

Educational actors (teachers and professionals in the field) show a null impact on field of study selection, suggesting that their advice also orients students equally into both conventional and nonconventional fields. While this non-impact indicates that teachers and professionals in the field are guiding students into a wide range of choices, it also indicates that little is being

---

common to all the indicators for that construct. Mathematically, it is best to examine this relationship as if the indicators were factor loadings. The common variance of the indicators is then used to define the latent variable (Falk, 1987, p. 78-77, Lohmoller, 1984).

According to practice, indicators' loading weights greater than .55 are considered acceptable measures. Regarding the interpretation of the influences among the latent variables, a common procedure is to consider path results greater than .10 as important effects; those with weights .11 - .19 are considered moderate; and those greater than .20, substantial.

As will be seen in the figures to follow, the loadings of the manifest indicators for the graduate and the undergraduate student models behaved well, except for those related to school agents, which performed weakly at the graduate level.

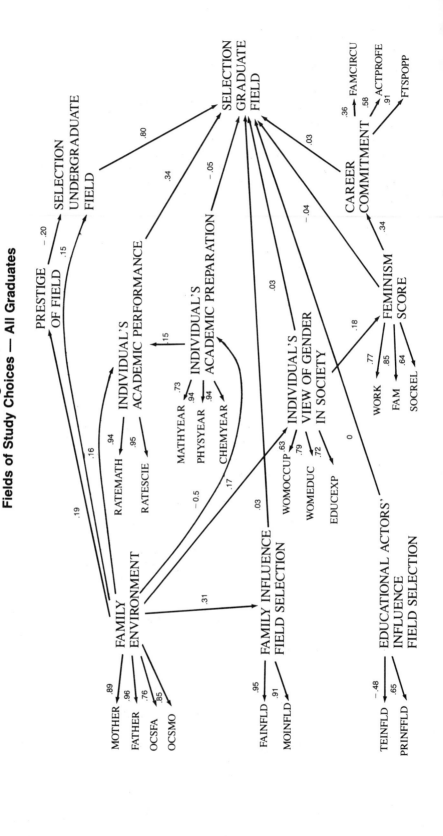

Figure B.
Fields of Study Choices — All Graduates

done on their part to give greater emphasis to the selection of nonconventional fields.

The family environment affects selecting a field because of the prestige it is supposed to have (.19), but feeling that a field is prestigious seems to lead to the avoidance of a nonconventional field (-.20). Why this is the case is unclear. The family environment also has a significant influence on the individual's view of gender in society, with better-off families sensitizing their children to perceive greater inequalities (.17), and these views, in turn, do influence subsequent levels of feminism (.18).

One of our key theoretical variables was the level of feminist attitudes. We expected to find a strong and positive influence of feminism upon both career commitment and the selection of a nonconventional graduate field. Our findings indicate that feminism indeed influences strongly the individual's commitment to a career (.34). This bears out theoretical expectations that individuals who believe men and women should be equal also will want to lead lives that are not bound by gender and family constraints. Thus, these individuals will presumably be committed to working full time in their jobs, to being active professionals, and to creating family situations that do not constrain them. The surprising finding, however, is that career commitment does not seem to lead to the selection of nonconventional fields (path coefficient of .03). Contrary to theoretical expectations, feminism does not exert an influence on the selection of type of graduate field. Its effects are insignificant even though they show a negative effect (-.04). Persons with a high level of feminism, then, move into both conventional and nonconventional fields.

A plausible explanation for the negative impact of the feminist score on field of study choices is that graduate students in nonconventional fields have little time for extracurricular activities. The earlier bivariate analyses, in fact, showed that students in conventional fields tended to know more about gender issues and to have a greater awareness of gender in society than students in nonconventional fields.

It is not that the feminism score has a negative impact on the choice of nonconventional field of study. Rather, those who make such a choice do so primarily on the basis of their ability in math and sciences. Once students are involved in math and science-related fields, these become absorbing activities which allow the students little time to develop broader interests.

There is a significant impact of selection of undergraduate field upon the selection of graduate field, as undergraduate field selection has a path coefficient of .80 — by far the strongest in the model — upon graduate field selection. The selection of the undergraduate field of study is the only one of seven variables in the model that directly and substantially influences the selection of field at the graduate level. The other six variables do not make a significant difference, showing small path coefficients ranging from .01 to .08.

In this regard, it should be noted that the selection of fields at the college level has a very stable character, as shifts among fields by degree of conventionality are few. This can be observed in **Table 74**, whose distribution produces a correlation of .81 (p = .001).

Table 74

Shifts in Field of Study Choice by Degree of Conventionality Between the Undergraduate and the Graduate Levels — All Graduate Students (Absolute Numbers)

Graduate Level	Undergraduate Level				
	0	1	2	3	4
0	75	5	2	—	—
1	26	35	10	6	3
2	7	13	105	7	1
3	2	1	28	80	4
4	1	1	4	4	21

Individuals in highly conventional fields for women (those having a score of 0) may move into slightly less conventional ones, but the numbers of those who do so is very small; most of them (75 out of 111) stay in their conventional field and none eventually moves into less conventional fields with scores of 3 and 4. Likewise, those in the most unconventional fields (those having a score of 4), tend to stay there, with only a few moving into conventional fields. The fields that register the greatest shift are those rated as having a score of 1, but a significant part of this shift is a movement from less conventionality toward more conventionality.

These data show how important field selections at the undergraduate level are. The possibility of additional course work or new interests being developed while the individuals are undergraduates is small. This is possibly due to the fact that prerequisites are necessary for many of the graduate courses that lead to nonconventional careers and the students who did not have previous exposure to pertinent subjects while in high school may not have the confidence or the skills necessary to take the prerequisites.

All together, this model shows a good fit, as it has a RMS covariance of .042 which indicates how well the overall model fits the raw data. The communality coefficient, which reflects the fit of the manifest variables (or outer model) is also good, having a coefficient of .67. Concerning the inner model (between the latent variables), the model produces an R square of .67, which is a high level of prediction. As noted earlier, much of the strong predictive value of the model comes from the influence that field selection at the undergraduate level has upon field selection at the graduate level. It should be noted that, unlike LISREL, the LVPLS program computes a small coefficient in cases of a good fit of data.[9]

Women Graduate Students

When applied only to the field of study choices of women in the sample, the model is slightly less precise than when applied to all graduate students, showing an RMS covariance of .043; however, it still shows a very good fit for the outer model (a coefficient of .68) and for the inner model (R square of .64).

The model (see **Figure C**) also shows the powerful effects of family environment upon daughters. This variable influences directly the selection of the undergraduate field (showing a path coefficient of .21), the individual's academic performance in math and science courses (path coefficient of .23), and the impact that the family will have in influencing field selection (.34). The effects of the family upon women students are greater than those over the combined sample (men and women together).

The direct effect of family environment upon selecting a field on the basis of its prestige is low (.09), unlike the case for all graduates (.19), which suggests that the importance of prestige for field selection operates in the case of men but not of women. On the other hand, prestige of field shows a significant but negative correlation with the selection of undergraduate field of study (-.23). This negative effect of prestige upon the selection of field of study, also detected in the model for all graduates, is difficult to explain.

The influence of family environment is moderate on the daughter's view of gender in society (.14), which, in turn, has a moderate association with feminist attitudes (.17).

The women's feminism score has a sizable impact on their career commitment (.53). Clearly, the greater the importance a woman places on women's rights to equality in work, family, and other social relations, the more she will want to work in her selected profession. This finding certainly follows theoretical expectations. Yet a high feminist score does not lead to selecting

---

[9]The RMS covariance (E,U) represents the root mean square of the covariance between the residuals of the manifest variables and the residuals of the latent variables. The lower the coefficient (i.e., the closer to zero), the better the model (Falk, 1987, pp. 84-85).

Figure C.
Fields of Study Choices — Women Graduates Only

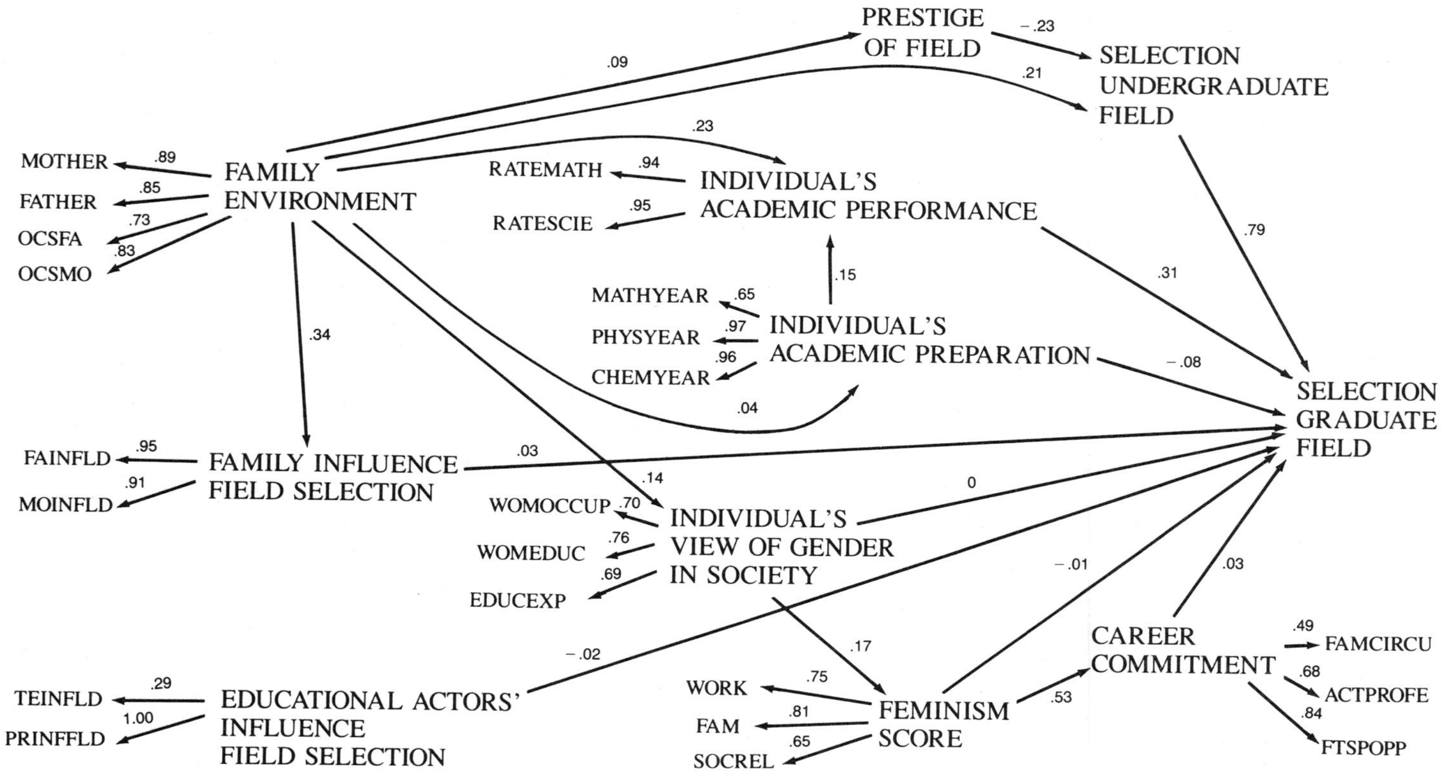

a nonconventional field (producing a path coefficient of -.01). Similarly, a high degree of career commitment does not influence the selection of a nonconventional field (.03). In other words, women may be strongly committed to their careers, even though these careers are in nursing, teaching, music, and other "feminine" disciplines.

As in the case for all the graduate students, the influence of family and school on the selection of a field does not lead to the selection of nonconventional field of studies among women (path coefficients of .03 and -.02, respectively). It is possible that the advice to explore specific nonconventional fields of study may come too late if women students have not previously been enrolled in math and natural sciences courses; or, the advice received may not encourage the selection of nonconventional fields of study. This latter interpretation may be valid when we recall (**Table 9**) that one of the most important sources of negative messages regarding NCF selection by women graduate students are parents and relatives (who constitute 49% of the sources of negative messages), and that teachers, advisors, and professionals are also a source of negative messages (14%).

Table 75 shows that the shifts from conventional to nonconventional fields are limited among women. The correlation between fields is strong, at .80 (p = .001). Among men, field shifts are also limited but less so than for women, producing a correlation coefficient of .74 (p = .001). These strong correlations support the notion of a cumulative effect — that choices at one level strongly influence choices at subsequent levels. In the case of women, this correlation may reflect a "cumulative disadvantage." In the case of men, it is also cumulative but along the lines of a positive advantage.

Most of the women in conventional fields will stay there; most of the women in nonconventional fields stay there but a good number regress by moving away from nonconventional to conventional fields.

Table 75
Shifts in Field of Study Choice by Degree of Conventionality Between Undergraduate and Graduate Levels — Women Graduate Students (Absolute Numbers)

Graduate Level	Undergraduate Level				
	0	1	2	3	4
0	66	5	2	–	–
1	25	31	6	5	2
2	6	8	83	5	–
3	1	1	15	35	1
4	1	–	3	3	9

The Undergraduate Students' Model

Given the poor performance of the prestige of field variable, it was deleted in the undergraduate students' model. The weights of the path coefficients in this model show a remarkable similarity to those manifested in the graduate student model, which increases the validity of our findings.

The family environment affects significantly the extent to which parents and relatives are heeded when a field of study is selected. The more educated the parents and the higher the status of their occupations, the greater the degree of influence they have upon the individual's field selection. Thus, the path coefficient from family environment to family influence on field selection shows a weight of .16 (see **Figure D**).

Family environment affects slightly the perceived performance of the undergraduate student in math and science (.11). As in the case of the graduate students, individual academic preparation has a sizable effect upon the individuals' academic performance (.22). The model also shows that it is not the number of years of exposure to math and science which prompt the individual to select nonconventional fields of study, but rather the self-perception of ability in those subjects. The former shows an insignificant effect (-.01); the latter, a sizable effect (.29).

Parents do not seem to affect the preparation of their children in math and science, but they affect their childrens' perception of performance in those areas. While parents are influential in shaping the field selection of their children, as in the case of graduate students, this influence does not produce the selection of nonconventional fields. Apparently, parents and relatives shape selection in either direction, in some cases guiding the students toward conventional fields, in others leading them into nonconventional fields. The influence of educational actors shows negative effects on the selection of a nonconventional field (-.12), which corroborates a previous finding from the bivariate analysis, namely that teachers and professionals in the field tend to be important influences, but more so in the selection of conventional than nonconventional fields.

The results show again that the individuals' view of gender in society does not lead to the selection of nonconventional fields (-.05). Feminist attitudes also do not have a strong effect on the selection of nonconventional fields; on the contrary, negative and weak effects seem to operate (-.14). Yet feminist attitudes do appear to have a sizable impact on career commitment (path coefficient of .27), a commitment that among undergraduates does seem to influence the selection of a nonconventional field (path = .11).[10]

---

[10]In all, the undergraduate field of study choice model has a relatively low explanatory power, producing an R square of .14. However, it offers a good communality coefficient (.59) and a good fit for the overall data (.048).

Figure D.
Fields of Study Choices — All Undergraduates

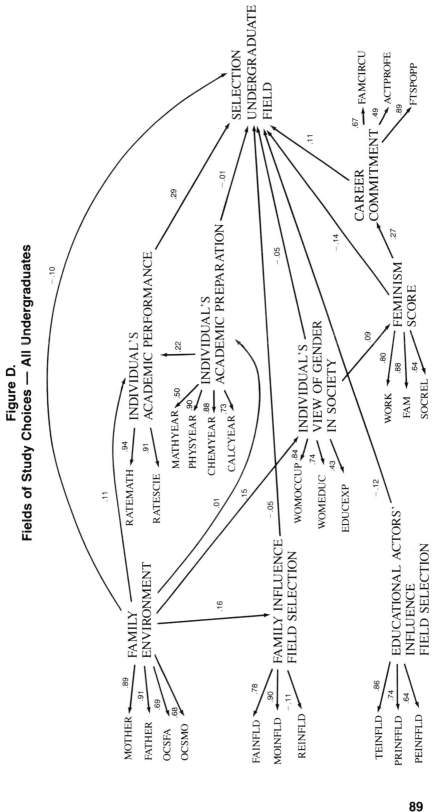

Women Undergraduate Students

When the field of study choice model is applied to women only, some differences are obtained even though no major departures emerge compared with the model for the combined group (see **Figure E**).

Family environment continues to have an insignificant direct effect on field of study choice (.01), although it has a substantive impact on the influence that parents and relatives will have on field selection by the individual (.12).

Among women undergraduates, there is no significant impact of the family environment upon the individual's perceived academic performance. But the impact of the individual's academic preparation upon perceived performance is slightly stronger among women (.25) than among the population as a whole (.22). Likewise, the impact of academic performance upon the selection of undergraduate fields is stronger among women (.33) than among the population as a whole (.29); the path coefficient of .33 is the strongest detected in the model. This finding confirms that for women, more so than for men, the most important reasons for selecting nonconventional fields are competence in the pertinent subjects and the objective of finding a good job after graduation (as seen in the previous bivariate analyses). Putting these two findings together, undergraduate women end up in nonconventional fields mainly because of their technical competence and the utilitarian aims they seek through these fields.

The young women's view of the impact of gender in society upon field selection has, surprisingly, a slightly negative effect (-.11), and their levels of feminism show a negative but insignificant impact (-.09), confirming the findings of the bivariate analyses showing that women in nonconventional fields tend to concentrate on strictly academic work and to have little exposure to women's courses or to participation in feminist groups. Such being the case, the women in nonconventional fields develop a limited understanding of gender relations in society.

The young women's level of feminism has a large impact upon career commitment (.51). The effect of feminism upon career commitment was also observed in the case of graduate women. A relevant comparison — and one we do not have — would be whether this relation holds among students who have not been abroad or among those who did not go to college. The impact of feminism on the career commitment expressed by women, not surprisingly, is much greater than among the undergraduate population as a whole (.27). In the case of women undergraduates, a high level of career commitment affects field selection negatively although weakly (-.10). The effects of career commitment on the selection of undergraduate field of study are puzzling. Although weak both among the general undergraduate population

Figure E.
Fields of Study Choices — Women Undergraduates Only

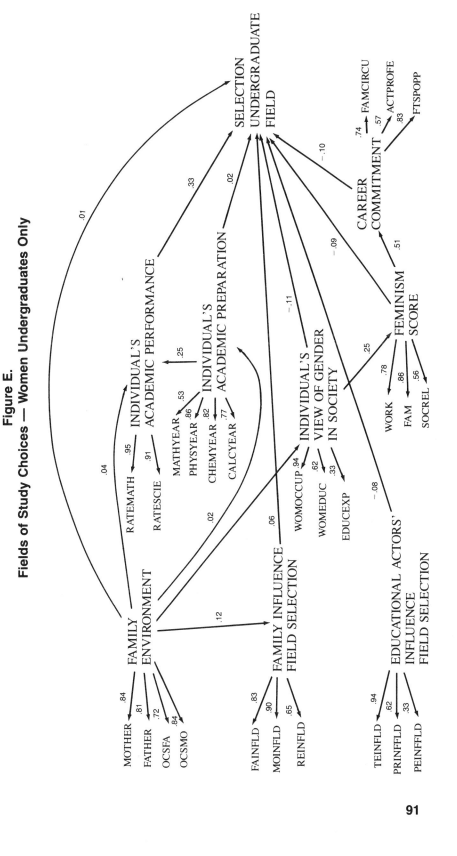

and female undergradute population, in the case of the former it has a positive effect (.11), but in the latter case it has a negative effect (-.10).[11]

In all, the selection of field of study at the undergraduate level proves elusive to capture. Family environment influences field selection but weakly and indirectly. Educational actors have a weak and negative influence. Only the student's perceived academic performance emerges as a strong predictor.

---

[11] This model has a similar total explanatory power as the model applied for the population as a whole. It reaches an R square of .13. Again, this model shows a good communality coefficient (.60) and a good fit for the overall data (.048).

VI.
The University
Experience of
Women in
Nonconventional
Fields

In this section, we explore the academic and social experiences of women in nonconventional fields to complement our understanding of the process of field selection. It has been observed that fields of study involve both a social and intellectual environment for the students. How are those women who cross conventional lines received in the academic arena? If women are outsiders in a particular field, what are the terms of their admission? What kind of identity do they establish? Knowing how women feel in their selected discipline after they enter it will help us further assess the socialization mechanisms within particular fields of study.

The experience as a female international student in a particular field occurs in three key arenas in addition to the classroom: the contact the student has with her professors, instructors, and peers outside of class; difficulties the student may experience in matters such as finances, ability in the English language, and sexual stereotyping; and involvement in departmental activities of an academic nature (this area is covered only in the case of graduate students).

Women Graduate Students in NCF

Contacts with Peers, Professors, and Instructors

The degree of contact with peers was measured by a structured item, ranging from having a "strong friendship" (scoring 4 points) to "no friendships" (scoring 1 point). The women in nonconventional fields, compared to their male counterparts, have fewer academic contacts with friends of their own sex and more social and academic contacts with friends of the opposite sex (see **Table 76**). The greater amount of contact with men probably encourages women to adopt the male perspective, and, perhaps, accounts, in part, for the low level of development of gender awareness among these women.

Table 76
Mean Level of Contact with Peers, Faculty, and Teaching Assistants
Reported by International Graduate Students

	NCF Women	CF Women	NCF Men
Social contact with friends own sex	2.66	2.60	2.64
Class contact with friends own sex	2.74	2.78	3.06**
Social contact with friends other sex	2.73	2.34**	2.19**
Class contact with friends other sex	2.88	2.59*	2.35**
Contact with faculty	2.36	2.60*	2.56*
Contact with TAs	2.43	2.37	2.14*
Ease approaching male professors	1.77	2.10*	1.86
Ease approaching female professors	1.80	1.88	1.85

  * T-test value significant at the .10 level.
 ** T-test value significant at the .05 level.
   The values in this and following tables derive from the comparison of women in nonconventional groups with the other two groups.

Contact with faculty and TAs was also measured through a structured item, ranging from "very close contact" (4 points) to "no contact" (1 point). In this matter, women in nonconventional fields appear to be at a clear disadvantage vis-a-vis men, having markedly fewer contacts with faculty. Both CF and NCF women have more contact than do men with teaching assistants, which may indicate that women receive less knowledgeable support in their studies. Compared even to CF women, NCF women have less contact with faculty members and report more problems in approaching male professors. The picture that emerges is that NCF women have least contact with faculty and feel least at ease in approaching them.

Difficulties in their Studies

Here we want to focus on some of the difficulties that may be peculiar to international students. We explored seven types of difficulty through a structured item, ranging from "very much difficulty" (4 points) to "no difficulty at all" (1 point) (see **Table 77**).

Table 77

Mean Level of Difficulties Experienced by International Graduate Students

Difficulties	NCF Women	CF Women	NCF Men
Financial issues: scholarships, loans, tuition remission	2.15	2.62*	2.20
Fluency/mastery of the English language	2.03	2.30	2.03
Mastery of math subjects	1.79	1.56	1.54*
Faculty prejudices about the capabilities of Third World students	1.77	1.97	1.68
Racism on the part of the faculty	1.73	1.73	1.59
Racism on the part of students	1.73	1.76	1.64
Sexual stereotypes on the part of the faculty	1.70	1.42*	1.17**

* T-test value statistically significant at the .05 level.
** T-test value statistically significant at the .001 level.

As can be observed, women in nonconventional fields have two substantially greater difficulties than the other two categories of students. They experience greater difficulty with math than men in nonconventional fields; this occurs despite their perception of themselves as having been very successful in math and science subjects while in high school. While the difficulty in math experienced by women in nonconventional fields was equivalent to "not very much difficulty," they do encounter more academic challenges than their male counterparts.

The presence of sexual stereotypes turned out to be the strongest source of difficulty for women in nonconventional fields; women in conventional fields do not experience these difficulties as much. While only 3 percent of the men report having encountered some difficulty with sexual stereotypes (none reports having had very much difficulty),16 percent of the female graduate students report having had some difficulty with sexual stereotypes and 2 percent of them state having had a great deal of difficulty with them (producing a chi-square significant at the .001 level). An analysis by the regional origin of the graduate students showed that difficulties with sexual stereotypes were felt by women from all four regions (Latin America, Asia, Africa, and the Middle East), though gender differences were statistically significant only in the case of Latin American and Asian students.

How did the students solve any of the above-mentioned difficulties? The response to this open-ended question indicated that the strategy adopted was usually one of avoiding the offending persons. By using this strategy, some female graduate students may come to lead a very isolated life.

Activities Within Their Department

We thought it was important to know what academic activities graduate students engaged in other than coursework. These activities were examined through a structured item that considered four types of involvement. The results are presented in terms of the percentages having engaged in a given activity.

Table 78
Engagement in Academic Activities Outside Coursework (in Percentages)

Type of Involvement	NCF Women	CF Women	NCF Men
As a teaching assistant	51	42	46
As a research assistant	42	13*	52
Has written joint papers with others in department	17	8	29*
Has given workshops with others in department	3	11	6

* Chi-square value significant at the .05 level.

The data show, not surprisingly, that women in nonconventional fields participated more frequently as research assistants than those in conventional fields. The NCF women obtain fewer research assistantships than men, but the difference is not statistically significant.

One difference between men and women in nonconventional fields that is statistically significant concerns participation in the production of joint papers. NCF women clearly engage in fewer instances of collaborative work than NCF men. The experience of writing joint papers is valuable on two counts: first, it affords students an invaluable research experience; second, it introduces the students to a network of other researchers, permits participation in meetings, and leads to publications that often accompany the production of a joint paper. Women, unfortunately, have limited access to this experience. Why does this occur? The systematic avoidance of women by male superiors has been documented in studies of women in administration in the United States (see for instance Shakeshaft, 1987). The reasons for avoidance are several: the belief that women will not take their careers as seriously as men will, the belief that men perform better than women, and the fear that a mentoring relationship with a person of the other sex may be interpreted as being a romantic/sexual liaison. While our data do not allow us to detect what reasons might be at work, the bottom line is that female students are not asked as often as male students to participate in collaborative intellectual efforts.

Undergraduate Women in NCF

Contacts with Peers, Professors, and Instructors

Overall, undergraduate NCF women are not different from other undergraduates, except perhaps that they tend to have more academic contacts with friends of the other sex, an early indication of their being in fields dominated by men and possibly the beginning of a socialization process that emphasizes technical rather than social concerns (**Table 79**).

NCF undergraduate women do not have disadvantages vis-a-vis men in contacting faculty and instructors. But when compared to CF women, the women in nonconventional fields experience substantially lower levels of contact with both faculty and TAs. These undergraduate women do not evince significant differences from the other groups in their ease of approaching male professors, but they report a much greater degree of ease in approaching female professors than do the other two groups. In all, undergraduate NCF women report lower levels of contact with instructors than graduate NCF women, but greater confidence in approaching male and female professors than the graduate students.

Table 79
Mean Level of Contact with Peers, Faculty, and Teaching Assistants
Reported by Undergraduate Students

	NCF Women	CF Women	NCF Men
Social contact with friends own sex	2.89	2.50	2.93
Class contact with friends own sex	2.84	2.85	3.03
Social contact with friends other sex	2.77	2.50	2.60
Class contact with friends other sex	2.75	2.60	2.54*
Contact with faculty	2.24	2.75**	2.36
Contact with TAs	2.36	2.78**	2.51
Ease approaching male professors	1.90	1.65	1.78
Ease approaching female professors	1.87	1.55	1.64**

  * T-test value statistically significant at the .10 level.
  ** T-test value statistically significant at the .05 level.

Difficulties in Their Studies

The difficulties reported by the NCF undergraduate women are different in three important respects from those of the other two groups. These students report more difficulties with the English language, which suggests that perhaps they excel in math and science at the expense of their abilities in language. They also report greater levels of difficulty with racism on the part of the faculty, a difference that is statistically significant when compared to the levels of difficulty reported by CF women. This difficulty was not reported by the NCF graduate-level women and we do not have an explanation for its greater incidence at the undergraduate level (see **Table 80**).

Table 80
Mean Level of Difficulties Experienced by International Undergraduate Students

Difficulties	NCF Women	CF Women	NCF Men
Financial issues: scholarships, loans, tuition remission	2.58	2.83	2.59
Fluency/mastery of the English language	2.19	2.00	1.90*
Mastery of math subjects	1.65	2.00*	1.62
Faculty prejudices about the capabilities of Third World students	1.88	1.78	1.86
Racism on the part of the faculty	1.83	1.22**	1.74
Racism on the part of students	2.19	1.88	2.04
Sexual stereotypes on the part of the faculty	1.78	1.52	1.31**

* T-test value statistically significant at the .05 level.
** T-test value statistically significant at the .001 level.

As in the case of the graduate students, NCF undergraduate women report high levels of sexual stereotyping on the part of the faculty. This difficulty shows a statistically significant level of .001 and is by far the strongest difference between the undergraduate groups compared. Indeed, the level of difficulty with sexual stereotypes is higher at the undergraduate (a mean value of 1.78) than at the graduate level (a mean value of 1.70). A comparison by regional origin showed that difficulties with sexual stereotypes were felt by all women, with statistically significant differences reported in the case of Asian, Latin American, and Middle Eastern students.

Altogether, women in nonconventional fields of study experience more academic isolation than women in conventional fields and men in nonconventional fields. They tend to communicate less with their professors, feel less at ease in contacting either male or female professors, and are invited less often than men to participate in the production of joint research papers. Moreover, women in nonconventional fields are subject to stereotyping that leads them into further isolation from others. This academic experience is certainly not one that promotes cognitive and personal growth in social areas; rather, it is an experience that fosters the development of technicians to the detriment of the creation of assertive, socially aware individuals.

VII. General Conclusions

Field of study choices emerge as decisions that do not occur overnight. They are the product of long years during which many "significant others" play a role. Once made, however, these decisions are permanent: our study found a remarkable consistency between graduate and undergraduate field of study selections, with few shifts between the baccalaureate and the advanced degree.

Since math and science performance have a strong impact on the selection of nonconventional fields, it can be argued that these competencies — and thus many of the preferences for fields associated with these competencies — develop early in life. Our data indicate that high school performance in math and science is a strong determinant of future field selection, but we cannot determine whether the necessary level of performance is already achieved in junior high school or even primary school.

Because field of study choices are embedded in everyday activities and social interaction, no single actor dominates the process. Parents emerge as important adults in guiding the career choices of children. Undeniably, the family has a strong impact on the individual given the frequency and closeness of interactions between family and individual and its ability to grant and withhold rewards. The father is particularly important in orienting daughters toward nonconventional fields, a consistent finding for women at both the graduate and undergraduate levels. Why are the fathers so influential? This might be a possible manifestation of the power of patriarchy. If men have more power than women, they are naturally seen as more important than women; thus fathers may have greater influence on children than mothers, even though those mothers may hold high occupational status, as was the case in our student sample. Mothers do not appear to play a pervasive role, perhaps because women — even as mothers — have less prestige and authority than men. In a few cases, however, supportive mothers seem to be particularly important in orienting daughters toward nonconventional fields.

But parents, along with relatives and friends, also provide messages that dissuade women from entering nonconventional fields. Dissuasion messages are subtle mechanisms of exclusion. A large number of parental messages for women are based on stereotypes and norms of what constitutes women's "proper" roles and responsibilities in society. Stereotypes are powerful means of conveying ideological information and thus serve simultaneously the functions of socialization and control of dominated groups (Cole, 1989). Given the continual nature of the contact with parents, it can be surmised that this influence affects considerably their children's definitions of gender, work, education, and family.

The effect of school agents on field selection is mixed. When comparing women in conventional with those in nonconventional fields, teachers have a noticeable impact on field selection. It is greater than that of parents at the graduate level and similar at the undergraduate level. It is a troublesome finding, however, that teachers play conservative roles in field of study guidance, a finding observed with respect to both graduate and undergraduate women. Counselors, despite formal responsibilities in career guidance, actually have very little influence on field of study choices. The influence of the mass media, in fact, is greater than the influence attributed to counselors. In spite of this, counselors seem to be more progressive than teachers in leading women into nonconventional fields, especially at the undergraduate level. At the graduate level, their influence has been forgotten. Professionals in the field have a sizable influence, but it operates mainly toward the selection of conventional fields of study.

The findings clearly demonstrate that competency in math and science has strong repercussions on the selection of nonconventional fields, for women as well as men. For women, this influence is stronger than for men at the undergraduate level but slightly less so at the graduate level. We interpret this to mean that if women enter fields which are not "appropriate" for women, then they have to overcompensate for the defiance of social norms by possessing excellent or above-average technical skills. The findings indicate that although *preparation* (years of study) in math and science courses does not have a direct impact on field selection, it has an important indirect effect through its persistent influence on the individual's *performance* in math and science. The longer a student has been exposed to math and science, the more highly the student evaluates her or his competence in that subject. While we find a strong association between individuals' academic performance in math and science and their selection of nonconventional

100

fields, we are unable to explain what accounts for individuals' exposure to and good performance in math and science in the first place.

The family environment, which has a powerful impact on making parents influential in field selection, proves to have an insignificant role upon individuals' academic preparation, a consistent finding across graduate and undergraduate students, both male and female. On the other hand, the family environment has a significant and positive impact on individuals' academic performance in math and science, particularly among female graduate students. Why does the home environment influence the perception of performance in math and science? It may be that in a home environment in which parents have high levels of education and are in professional fields that call for rather high levels of math ability, children learn to be comfortable with math skills and scientific explanations. They may, therefore, be less inclined to take courses in these subjects because they feel they do not need them. By contrast, for individuals coming from less favorable home environments, exposure to several years of math and science appears to act as a strong prerequisite for developing competencies in math and science.

We had conjectured that a high awareness of gender inequalities in society might lead female students to select nonconventional fields. This hypothesis was repeatedly disconfirmed in the causal model tested. Neither for graduate nor undergraduate women did views of gender in society significantly affect field of study choices. In fact, women in nonconventional fields persistently attained scores that reflected not only a low awareness of gender inequalities in society — which we called a gender naive view — but also had lower scores than women in conventional fields.

Likewise, we had posited that women in nonconventional fields would be characterized by higher levels of feminism than their counterparts in conventional fields of study, and that levels of feminism would significantly influence field of study choices. Again, the causal model tested consistently showed that this is not the case. The bivariate analysis showed that women in nonconventional fields had higher levels of feminism than men in those fields, but they had lower levels of feminism than women in conventional fields. Obviously, forces other than gender awareness — and other than defiance of social norms regarding women's appropriate roles — drive field of study choices.

Feminist attitudes did have a substantial influence in leading women to want to work outside of the home. In fact, this impact is one of the highest in our causal model and is equally high for graduate and undergraduate women (with path coefficients of .53 and .51, respectively). Yet commitment to work does not have an influence on field selection, as women interested in conventional or nonconventional fields may desire with equal strength to participate in the labor force.

Why do women in nonconventional fields have low levels of awareness of gender conditions and problems in society? Various reasons may be considered. One is that by entering nonconventional fields, women are coopted into defining problems in technical terms, not in terms of social relations. It may be that they learn that being objective and scientific means to ignore "personal" problems. Another possible explanation is that women in nonconventional fields, even more than men in those fields, take little part in courses beyond their specializations. They also have little time to participate in extracurricular activities such as conferences, meetings, and joining feminist groups. All of these activities are missing in the lives of graduate and undergraduate women in nonconventional fields. Consequently, they have limited exposure to feminist knowledge and ideas. Whatever they learn is gained basically through informal, and thus sporadic, contacts. As a result, these women become students committed to their fields but with little understanding of and commitment to social change.

Rossi notes that forms of gender inequality range from "explicit legal statute to informal social pressure" (1964, p. 175). The presence of sexual stereotypes in the experience of the international female students, particularly at the graduate level when they are vulnerable given their low numbers and rather alienated student life, must be construed as a perverse yet subtle manifestation of inequality.

We were surprised to find that despite the high levels of effort required for advanced studies in nonconventional fields, women in these fields give priority to family over career. Women in nonconventional fields of study want, above all, to be married and to have families. These are objectives that nobody questions. Unfortunately, these women subscribe to traditional definitions of the wife and mother, which generally signify a willingness to accept constraints derived from marriage and family responsibilities and to take for themselves the residual opportunities. This acceptance of traditional definitions of mother and wife also leads them to imagine working part-time and to demonstrate little political activism — expectations and attitudes that do not suggest good prospects for future leadership on their part.

The fact that women in nonconventional fields are willing to let their husband's career take priority over their own means that they do not anticipate for themselves strong professional leadership roles. It has been noted that the sex role socialization works simultaneously to weaken women and to further strengthen men. Bryson notes:

Men, on the other hand, expect that they will not only have to be financially independent, but will probably have others dependent on them. The expectation of man's superior, provider status means that women are unlikely to achieve their full potential, at least in the economic arena. Since in capitalist societies this is the key institutional sphere, the implications of this must not be underestimated. The whole process results, to quote Bell and Newby again, "in a degree of ideological hegemony over women so that they continue to accept their subordinate position as natural and desirable and the superior power of men as legitimate." Of course, we must not make the mistake of treating this hegemony as complete, it certainly never has been: the feminist movement provides the most obvious example of its limits." (1983, p. 145.)

The most defining characteristic of women in nonconventional fields is not awareness of social and economic problems affecting women or insistence on their rights to a professional career but their strong ability in math and science. In a previous study of women in nonconventional careers, Rossi asserted that the "increase of women scientists is ... one of the many socially desirable changes" (1967, p. 627). This may be so, but if the future women scientists have not been able to develop a wider and more progressive range of social attitudes, their increased numbers may not mean much.

It could be argued, however, that as women reach a critical mass in NCF, gender conflicts for positions and definitions of field may ensue and that this will create a major opportunity for change. This idea, that liberal (and even conservative) women will bring about change, is also shared by noted feminist Eisenstein, who in *The Radical Future of Liberal Feminism* (1980) predicts that as more women enter the workforce, they will expose various oppressive features of both patriarchy and capitalism.

Some Policy Implications

The study found that a good number of international female students select nonconventional fields while in this country. This suggests that planners in U.S. universities could further promote this tendency by increasing the access of female students to a wider set of course offerings. Also, they could provide more courses in math and science to develop among female students greater feelings of competence.

It would seem imperative to accompany such efforts with special measures to render women in nonconventional fields more progressive along gender lines. Again, university planners should seek either ways of mainstreaming the curriculum, so that coverage of gender issues permeates more disciplinary lectures and subsequent class discussions, or offer gender courses that are part of the core programs of study, so that exposure to them is much more widespread. U.S. universities also need to offer greater opportunities to women in nonconventional fields for contact with faculty and for access to extracurricular activities. These recommendations coincide with those offered by Komarovsky (1985), after seeing the modest career aspirations of American college women in the early 80s.

The findings indicate that the university environment needs to be improved substantially to provide a friendlier and more supportive environment toward women. The presence of sexual stereotypes can operate as a considerable source of discouragement and needs to be addressed explicitly. This finding suggests that workshops for professors and instructors on the subjects of sexual stereotypes and sexual discrimination may be highly advisable.

An unexpected finding — and one that can be turned around to the advantage of women — is the fact that women in conventional fields have both high levels of feminism and greater exposure to feminist ideas. This being the case, they may have a substantial potential for becoming agents of change. These women, for instance, could play an important role in changing the curriculum of departments that maintain conservative orientations, such as education and sociology. An advisable action, then, may be to target these women for more systematic exposure to social and gender problems and to strategies for their modification.

Areas for Further Research

It would seem extremely useful to trace a number of these international women upon their return to their countries and entrance into the labor force. Does their professional experience change their understanding of gender inequalities in society? As they live in the relatively sheltered university environment, does their level of consciousness rise?

In this regard, three foci of research come to mind. First, it would also be important to know how women in nonconventional occupations rate themselves in terms of personal and professional satisfaction compared with women in conventional fields. In particular, it would be useful to know in what ways women in nonconventional occupations feel they are making a social and/or a professional contribution.

Second, the study assessed expectations regarding family relationships, as these women will make choices between career and family. These expectations did not augur increased autonomy by women. It would be useful, however, to verify whether these expectations become a reality years later.

Third, the impact of sexually stereotypic messages upon women in nonconventional fields deserves greater exploration. As noted earlier, sexual stereotypes were identified as the largest difficulty experienced by women in their studies. It would be important to know in what forms these stereotypes manifest themselves, what impact they have on student morale, performance, and persistence in nonconventional fields, and what could be done to eliminate or reduce their occurrence.

Most works of inequality in the labor force concentrate on occupational segregation, not field of study choices. The examination of occupational segregation focuses on the product rather than the process by which this segregation became possible. We believe that this study, by focusing on field selection — the key precursor to occupational segregation — has provided us important insights not easily visible after individuals assume specific positions. The examinations of individuals' choices of fields enables us to see influences while they are still fresh and ongoing in the individuals' mind, so the process of reconstruction is more precise as it is closer to individual agency. The process of gender ideology transmission excludes women from certain fields, and even when women select to enter nonconventional fields, they give priority to husbands and marriage. The findings in our study certainly indicate the need for corrective action, but they also underscore that this action must start earlier — at the school rather than at the marketplace. Beginning at the marketplace is simply too late.

The concern for gender equality that was vibrant during the 1975-1985 U.N. Decade for Women made many women aware that a vital arena for social transformation was located at the higher education level. Initially, women wanted equal access. Then, we realized that it was necessary to move into male-dominated fields once access was obtained. Today, a further realization emerges: it is not enough to bring our bodies and talents to fields previously reserved for men. It is also necessary to bring with us the vision and courage that will enable us to transform those fields and the society they are meant to serve.

References

Angrist, Shirley and Elizabeth Almquist. *Careers and Contingencies.* New York: Dunellen, 1975.

Anyon, Jean. Intersections of Gender and Class: Accomodation and Resistance by Working-Class and Affluent Females to Contradictory Sex-Role Ideologies. In S. Walker and L. Barton (eds.), *Gender, Class, and Education.* London: The Falmer Press, 1983.

Ashton, David and M. Maguire. "Young Women in the Labor Market: Stability and Change." In Rosemary Deem (ed.), *Schooling for Women's Work.* London: Routledge & Kegan Paul, 1980, pp. 112-125.

Becker, Gary. *The Economics of Discrimination.* Chicago: University of Chicago Press, 1971.

Bourdieu, P. and J. C. Passeron. *Reproduction in Education, Society, and Culture.* Beverly Hills: Sage Publications, 1977.

Bridges, Judith, and Mary Bower. "The Effects of Perceived Job Availability for Women in College Women's Attitudes Toward Prestigious Male-Dominated Occupations," *Psychology of Women Quarterly,* no. 9, 1985, pp. 265277.

Bryant, Clifton. *The Social Dimensions of Work.* Englewood Cliffs, New Jersey: Prentice-Hall, Inc., 1972.

Campbell, Paul and Suzanne Laughlin. *Climbing Toward Equality: The Postsecondary Advantage.* Colombus: The National Center for Research in Vocational Education, 1987, mimeo.

Clarricoates, Katherine. "The Importance of Being Ernest... Emma... Tom... Jane." In Rosemary Deem (ed.), *Schooling for Women's Work.* London: Routledge & Kegan Paul, 1980, pp. 26-41.

Cole, Mike (ed.). *The Social Contexts of Schooling.* London: The Falmer Press, 1989.

Connell, Robert. *Gender and Power.* Stanford: Stanford University Press, 1987.

Deaux, Kay. "From Individual Differences to Social Categories: Analysis of a Decade's Research on Gender," *American Psychologist,* no. 39, 1984, pp. 105-116.

Delphy, Christine. *The Main Enemy: A Materialist Analysis of Women's Oppression.* London: Women's Research and Resources Centre, 1977.

Douvan, Elizabeth and Joseph Adelson. *The Adolescent Experience.* New York: John Wiley, 1966.

Eisenstein, Zillah. *The Radical Future of Liberal Feminism.* New York: Longman, 1980.

Elliott, Jane and Chris Powell. Young Women and Science: Do We Need More Science? *British Journal of Sociology of Education,* vol. 8, no. 3, 1987, pp. 277-286.

Evans, Terry D. (1982) Being and Becoming: Teachers' Perceptions of Sex-Roles and Actions Toward Their Male and Female Pupils, *British Journal of Sociology of Education,* vol. 3, no. 2, pp. 127-143.

Falk, R. Frank. *A Primer for Soft Modeling.* Berkeley: Institute of Human Development, University of California at Berkeley, April 1987.

Fassinger, Ruth. "A Causal Model of College Women's Career Choice," *Journal of Vocational Behavior,* vol. 27, 1985, pp. 123-153.

Gaskell, Jane. "The Reproduction of Family Life: Perspectives of Male and Female Adolescents," *British Journal of Sociology of Education,* vol. 4, no. 1, 1983.

Gilligan, Carol. *In a Different Voice: Psychological Theory and Women's Development.* Cambridge: Harvard University Press, 1982.

Hartmann, Heidi. "Capitalism, Patriarchy, and Job Segregation by Sex." In Z. Eisenstein (ed.), *Capitalist Patriarchy and the Case for Socialist Feminism.* New York: Monthly Review Press, 1979.

Hartmann, Heidi. *Women, Work, and Wages.* Washington, D.C.: National Academy Press, 1981.

Hartsock, Nancy. "Political Change: Two Perspectives on Power." In The Quest Staff (eds.), *Building Feminist Theory.* New York: Longman, 1981.

Institute of International Education. *IIE News Release.* New York: Institute of International Education, December 1, 1986.

Institute of International Education. *Open Doors: 1986/87. Report on International Education Exchange.* New York: Institute of International Education, 1987.

Institute of International Education. *Open Doors: 1988/89. Report on International Education Exchange.* New York: Institute of International Education, 1989.

Komarovsky, Mirra. *Women in College.* New York: Basic Books, Inc., Publishers, 1985.

Lohmoller, Jan-Bernd. *LVPLS Program Manual. Version 1.6.* Koln: Universitat zu Koln, 1984.

Neddings, Nel. *Caring. A Feminist Approach to Ethics and Moral Education.* Berkeley: University of California Press, 1984.

Powers, Mary and Joan Holmberg. "Occupational Status Scores: Changes Introduced by the Inclusion of Women." In Mary Powers (ed.), *Measures of Socioeconomic Status. Current Issues.* Boulder: Westview Press, Inc., 1982.

Ram, Rati. "Sex Differences in the Labor Market Outcomes of Education." In Gail Kelly and Carolyn Elliott (eds.), *Women's Education in the Third World. Comparative Perspectives.* Albany: State University of New York Press, 1982, pp. 203-227.

Reiffers, J., A. Cartapanis, W. Experton, and J. Fuguet *Transnational Corporations and Endogenous Development.* Paris: UNESCO, 1982.

Rentz, M. Diplomats in Our Backyard. *Newsweek,* February 16, 1987.

Reskin, Barbara and Heidi Hartmann (eds.). *Women's Work, Men's Work. Sex Segregation on the Job.* Washington, D.C.: National Academy Press, 1986.

Rosenberg, Morris. "Which Significant Others?" *American Behavioral Scientist,* vol. 16, no. 6, July/August 1973, pp. 829-860.

Rossi, Alice. "Sex Equality: The Beginning of Ideology." In Betty Roszak and Theodore Roszak (eds.), *Masculine/Feminine. Readings in Sexual Mythology and the Liberation of Women.* New York: Harper & Row Publishers, 1964.

Rossi, Alice. Women in Science: Why So Few? In Athena Theodore (ed.), *The Professional Woman.* Cambridge: Schenkman Publishing Company, Inc., 1971, pp. 612-628.

Schoenmaker, Linda. "Gender and College-Bound Adolescent Career-Field Choices: An Exploratory Analysis." Doctoral dissertation, University of Southern California, May 1988.

Shakeshaft, Charol. *Women in Educational Administration.* Newbury Park: Sage Publications, 1987.

Siegel, Sidney. *Nonparametric Statistics for the Behavioral Sciences.* New York: McGraw-Hill Book Company, 1956.

Strober, Myra. "Toward a General Theory of Occupational Sex Segregation: The Case for Public School Teaching." In Barbara Reskin (ed.), *Sex Segregation in the Workplace: Trends, Explanations, Remedies.* Washington, D.C.: National Academy Press, 1984.

Theodore, Athena (ed.). *The Professional Woman.* Cambridge: Schenkman Publishing Company, Inc., 1971.

Theodore, Athena. "The Professional Woman: Trends and Prospects." In Athena Theodore (ed.), *The Professional Woman.* Cambridge: Schenkman Publishing Company, Inc., 1971, pp. 1-35.

Treiman, Donald. *Occupational Prestige in Comparative Perspective.* New York: Academic Press, 1977.

UNESCO. *Education Statistics. Latest Year Available.* Paris: UNESCO, 1986.

Wiegers, Rebeca and Irene Friezer. "Gender, Female Traditionality." *Psychology of Women Quarterly,* no. 2, 1977, pp. 125-137.

Zikopoulos, Marianthi and Elinor Barber. *Choosing Schools from Afar.* New York: Institute of International Education, 1986.

Appendix A

Letter of Introduction and Questionnaire for Graduate Students

Dear International Student:

This is to request your *participation* in a study which seeks to find out how *international students* choose their fields of study and what factors operate to facilitate or hamper these choices. The study focuses especially on the possible differences between the experiences of women and men. It also seeks to include information about the effects on your career decisions of your experience in a U.S. university. We hope this study will produce useful policy recommendations to help future international students.

I would much appreciate it if you would fill out the attached questionnaire. Your response is extremely important to the success of the study because you are a part of a selected sample representing the entire population of international students in this country. I have tried to keep to a minimum the time needed to complete the questionnaire; it should take approximately 30 minutes. As you respond to the questions, imagine yourself having a silent dialogue with me. You will see that we shall cover various aspects of your experiences in your home country and as an international student. Your answers will be kept totally confidential. All reports will be made in terms of statistical averages to prevent any identification of individuals. When the study is completed, the results will be widely disseminated, and a copy will be sent to staff at your university.

This study has the endorsement of the Office for International Students and Scholars of Michigan State University, and is being sponsored by the Institute of International Education. Please answer the questionnaire in the next three days and consider *all* of the questions. Use the enclosed self-addressed and stamped envelope to return the questionnaire.

Thank you for your important and generous contribution.

Nelly P. Stromquist
Associate Professor

PLEASE NOTE THAT THIS QUESTIONNAIRE IS PRINTED ON BOTH SIDES OF THE PAGE. LET US BEGIN:

1. What is your country of origin?_____

2. Place where born: rural area_____   urban area_____

3. Age (check one): 18-22__ 23-27__ 28-32__ 33-37__ 38-42__
    43-above__

4. Sex: ( ) Female   ( ) Male

5. Highest degree achieved:
    ( ) Bachelor's degree
    ( ) Master's degree

    Field of degree (please specify):_____

    Where obtained? (check one): ( ) home country   ( ) U.S.
    ( ) other (specify)_____

6. Degree program in which you are currently enrolled:
    ( ) M.A.   ( ) M.S.   ( ) Doctorate
    ( ) Other (please specify):_____

7. Field of Study (specify) :_____ Specialization (specify) :_____

8. How firm is your choice of field of study?
    ( ) Very firm   ( ) Moderately firm   ( ) Not very firm
    ( ) Will probably change

9. When did you develop an interest in your current field of study?
    (check one) ( ) Before coming to this country.
                ( ) After coming to this country.

10. How did you learn about your current field?_____
    _____

11. Why did you select your field? Check all the reasons that apply.
    ( ) Field will lead to definite employment opportunities.
    ( ) It is a field that will not create conflict with future family
        responsibilities.
    ( ) It is a field whose content interests me very much regardless of
        occupational potential.
    ( ) The admission criteria for this field are not very rigorous.
    ( ) My family expects me to enter this field.
    ( ) Government or funding agency promoted the field.
    ( ) Other (please specify) _____

12. Were you ever interested in pursuing a different advanced program?
    ( ) Yes
    ( ) No
    If yes, why did you not select it?_____
    _____

13. What is the highest level of education you expect to achieve?
    ( ) Master's degree
    ( ) Doctorate

14. Probable field and specialization if further studies are desired (please specify):
    _____

15. Why did you want to study in the United States?
    _____
    _____

16. Is your field of study available in the universities of your country?
    ( ) Yes (Answer A)
    ( ) No
    ( ) I don't know

    A. If you had stayed in your country would you have selected the same field of study?
       ( ) Yes
       ( ) No
       If no, why not?_____

17. Is your specialization within your field of study available in your country?
    ( ) Yes   ( ) No   ( ) I don't know

18. When did you select your specialization?
    ( ) Before coming to this country
    ( ) While a student in this country

19. What factors led you to select your current specialization?
    ( ) Advice from professors
    ( ) Courses on the topic I took in this university
    ( ) Courses on the topic I took in a university in my country
    ( ) Other (specify)_____

20. How would you describe your field of study as it exists in your country?
    ( ) A field that traditionally attracts mostly women
    ( ) A field that traditionally attracts mostly men
    ( ) It attracts men and women in similar proportions
    ( ) I don't know

21. Are there women in professions related to your field of study in your country?
( ) Many   ( ) None
( ) Some   ( ) I don't know
( ) Only a few

22. Was the decision to pursue your current field of study mostly yours or was it mostly influenced by others?
( ) Mostly my decision
( ) Mostly influenced by others

23. How important was each of the following persons in influencing your choice of field of study? Check the appropriate column for each.

	very important	important	somewhat important	not important
• Father	_____	_____	_____	_____
• Mother	_____	_____	_____	_____
• Teacher(s)	_____	_____	_____	_____
• School counselor	_____	_____	_____	_____
• Professionals in the field	_____	_____	_____	_____
• College peers	_____	_____	_____	_____
• Relatives/siblings	_____	_____	_____	_____
• Mass media	_____	_____	_____	_____
• Other (please specify)				
_____	_____	_____	_____	_____

24. Did anybody try to discourage you?
( ) No
( ) Yes   If yes, who? (please specify)_____

25. What reasons were given?_____

26. Prior to your choice of field of study, what kinds of activities did you engage in to prepare yourself for that choice? Check *as many as* apply.
( ) Talked to professors about personal preferences and job opportunities
( ) Talked to career counselor about personal preferences and job opportunities
( ) Read books about professions and careers
( ) Talked with professionals in my chosen field
( ) No preparation took place
( ) Other (specify)_____

27. Can you identify a particular experience as an undergraduate student that significantly influenced your choice of field?_____

28. What do you like **best** about the field you are in? Rank the three most attractive features, with "1" as the most attractive.
( ) The discipline is of great interest to me.
( ) The discipline requires math/science skills.
( ) The discipline requires verbal skills/English.
( ) The field offers many possibilities for finding a job.
( ) The field has high prestige.
( ) I like its competitive atmosphere.
( ) The field is not dominated by one sex.

29. What do you like **least** about your field? Rank the three least attractive features, with "1" as the most *unattractive*.
( ) The coursework is very difficult.
( ) The field offers few possibilities for finding a job.
( ) The field requires math/science skills.
( ) The field requires verbal skills/English.
( ) The field has low prestige.
( ) I dislike its competitive atmosphere.
( ) The field is dominated by one sex.
( ) There is nothing I dislike about my field.

30. Is there anyone in your field whom you know personally and whom you consider as an example to follow?
( ) Yes
( ) No

31. If yes, is this person ( ) a woman or ( ) a man?

32. Is this person from your country?
( ) Yes
( ) No

33. Why do you consider this person an example to follow?
_____
_____

34. Did you know this person before making your choice of field of study?
( ) Yes
( ) No

35. In your view, what is the **most** important feature of the occupation you plan to have?
( ) good salary
( ) chance to help others
( ) chance to be my own boss
( ) steady employment
( ) interesting work
( ) advancement possibilities

36. Do you anticipate obstacles as you seek to enter an occupation in your field?
( ) Yes
( ) No

37. If yes, what kinds of obstacles might emerge? Please elaborate.
_____
_____

NOW WE HAVE SOME QUESTIONS ABOUT YOUR EXPERIENCE AT THIS UNIVERSITY.

University currently enrolled_____

38. How long have you been at this university?
_____years_____months

39. Have you studied elsewhere in the United States?
( ) No
( ) Yes   If yes, how many years?_____months_____
Where?_____

40. Who pays for most of your education?

( ) Family   ( ) U.S. government
( ) This university   ( ) Myself
( ) Home government   ( ) Other_____

41. How would you describe your friendships with peers of your **own sex** at this university?
Check the column that best describes these friendships:

	strong	moderate	weak	no friendship
In the area of social events	_____	_____	_____	_____
In the area of classwork/ studies	_____	_____	_____	_____

42. How would you describe your friendships with peers of the **other sex** at this university?
Check the column that best describes these friendships:

	strong	moderate	weak	no friendship
In the area of social events	_____	_____	_____	_____
In the area of classwork/ studies	_____	_____	_____	_____

116

43. How would you describe your contacts with **faculty members** in your department?
    ( ) Very close
    ( ) Somewhat close
    ( ) Not very close
    ( ) No contact outside of class
    　　　Why is this so?_____

44. How would you describe your contacts with **teaching assistants** in your department?
    ( ) Very close
    ( ) Somewhat close
    ( ) Not very close
    ( ) No contact outside of class

45. In your department, have you taken or are you taking courses taught by female professors? (check one)
    ( ) Yes　　　( ) No

46. In your department, have you taken or are you taking courses in which female students serve as teaching assistants? (check one)
    ( ) Yes　　　( ) No

47. How difficult is it for you to approach the following people? Check the column that best describes your degree of difficulty:

	very difficult	somewhat difficult	not very difficult	not difficult at all
Male professors	_____	_____	_____	_____
Female professors	_____	_____	_____	_____

48. In which of the following activities have you participated in your department? Check as many as apply.
    ( ) As a teaching assistant
    ( ) As a research assistant
    ( ) Have written joint papers with a member/members of my department
    ( ) Have given workshops with a member of my department
    ( ) None of the above

49. How much support/advice regarding your current studies do you regularly get from the following persons?

	very much	some	little	very little	I don't request it
Professors	____	____	____	____	____
Academic program advisor	____	____	____	____	____
Foreign student advisor	____	____	____	____	____
Fellow American students	____	____	____	____	____
Fellow international students	____	____	____	____	____
Non-university friends	____	____	____	____	____

50. If you have had problems regarding your **studies**, how would you rate the advice/support received from the following people?

	very effective	somewhat effective	not very effective	ineffective	I haven't requested help
Academic program counselor	___	___	___	___	___
Foreign student advisor	___	___	___	___	___
Professors	___	___	___	___	___
Fellow American students	___	___	___	___	___
Fellow international students	___	___	___	___	___

51. If you hae had **personal problems** while attending this university, how would you rate the advice/support received from the following people?

	effective	somewhat effective	not very effective	ineffective	help not requested
Professors	___	___	___	___	___
Academic program counselor	___	___	___	___	___
Foreign student advisor	___	___	___	___	___
Fellow students	___	___	___	___	___
Non-university friends	___	___	___	___	___

52. Rate the degree of difficulty you have experienced at your university in the following matters.

	very much difficulty	some difficulty	not very much difficulty	no difficulty at all
Financial issues: tuition remission, scholarships, loans, etc.	___	___	___	___
Fluency/mastery of the English language	___	___	___	___
Mastery of math subjects	___	___	___	___
Faculty prejudices about the capabilities of Third World students	___	___	___	___
Racism on the part of the faculty	___	___	___	___
Racism on the part of the students	___	___	___	___
Sexual stereotypes on the part of the faculty	___	___	___	___
Other (please specify): _____	___	___	___	___

53. Generally, how have you solved these problems, if any?

_____

_____

54. Can you suggest any ways in which your university could improve its performance to help you to succeed in your field of study? Be as specific as possible.

_____
_____
_____

NOW WE HAVE SOME QUESTIONS ABOUT YOUR FAMILY AND YOUR EDUCATIONAL EXPERIENCE WHEN YOU LIVED IN YOUR OWN COUNTRY.

55. How many brothers do you have? _____

56. How many sisters do you have?_____

57. If you have older brothers and sisters who are studying in college or who already have a profession, please give their first name, field of study, sex, and age.

Name	Field of study	Sex	Age
_____	_____	___	___
_____	_____	___	___
_____	_____	___	___
_____	_____	___	___

58. Indicate your parent's **highest** level of education, by checking the appropriate column. (Answer this even if parent is dead.)

	incomplete primary	complete primary	incomplete secondary	complete secondary	Polytechnical/ incomplete higher edu.	B.A./ B.S.	M.A./ M.S. LL.B.	Ph.D M.D.
Mother's level of education	___	___	___	___	___	___	___	___
Father's level of education	___	___	___	___	___	___	___	___

Father's principal occupation/field_____
Title of father's position at work_____
Mother's principal occupation/field_____
Title of mother's position at work_____

59. If your mother does not now hold a paying job, has she ever worked outside the home? (including managing her own business or working in family business) (check one)
( ) Yes, she worked previously but not now
( ) No, she has never worked outside the home

60. If she has worked outside the home, what different jobs has she held? (please describe)
1 _____
2 _____

61. Please indicate how many **years** of the following you took in secondary school:

_____ math (including algebra, geometry and trigonometry)

_____ biology _____ chemistry

_____ physics _____ calculus

62. While in secondary school, your teachers were (check one):
( ) Mostly men
( ) Mostly women
( ) Equally men and women

63. Did you ever attend coeducational schools (serving both female and male students)? Please check all the statements that apply:
( ) I was never in coeducational school
( ) I was in coeducational school part of primary
( ) I was in coeducational school all of primary
( ) I was in coeducational school part of secondary
( ) I was in coeducational school all of secondary

64. In what type of institution did you study as an undergraduate?
( ) In a coeducational college/university
( ) In a one-sex only college/university

65. How would you rate yourself relative to your peers back in **secondary** school in math ability?
( ) highest 1% of the class
( ) highest 10% of the class
( ) above average
( ) average
( ) below average

66. How would you rate yourself to your peers back in **secondary** school in science ability?
( ) highest 1% of the class
( ) highest 10% of the class
( ) above average
( ) average
( ) below average

67. What was your undergraduate major?_____

68. What was your undergraduate minor?_____

69. And, reflecting on your **undergraduate** experience, how would you rate yourself compared to your peers in terms of academic achievement?
( ) above average
( ) average
( ) below average

70. If you worked for a wage or salary before coming to the university, what types of jobs have you held? Please specify. If no job for pay, circle "3"

    1 _____

    2 _____

    3 Did not work for pay before coming to university.

71. If you have worked before as a volunteer (a non-paid job), what types of jobs have you held? Please specify. If no volunteer jobs, circle "3"

    1 _____

    2 _____

    3 Did not work as a volunteer before coming to university.

PLEASE HELP US UNDERSTAND HOW YOU VIEW MARRIAGE AND CAREER OPTIONS. ANSWER ALL THE QUESTIONS BELOW, EVEN IF YOU ARE A MALE STUDENT.

72. *For graduate students who are single, only*: If your future spouse were opposed to your working after marriage, what would you do? Check *one* statement.

    ( ) Choose marriage and forget career.

    ( ) Choose marriage and hope that spouse will change mind after marriage.

    ( ) Choose marriage and try to change future spouse's mind before marriage.

    ( ) Choose career and forget marriage.

For graduate students who are married, only: How would you characterize your spouse's support of your future career? Check *one* statement.

    ( ) Very supportive of my career, spouse will, if necessary, give priority to job demands regarding location, schedules and travel.

    ( ) Very supportive of my career, but spouse's own career demands take priority.

    ( ) Very supportive of my career, all career moves between us have equal weight.

    ( ) Not very supportive of my career demands; sometimes this is a source of conflict at home.

    ( ) Not all supportive of my career; sometimes this undermines my career.

73. Do you expect the location and time requirements of your future occupation to conflict with family responsibilities?

    ( ) No, there will be no conflict.

    ( ) There will be a conflict but my family needs will take precedence over career needs.

    ( ) There will be a conflict but career needs will take precedence over family needs.

74. At this university, which of the following activities have you undertaken? Choose *as many as* apply:
    ( ) Attended courses dealing with women's issues.
    ( ) Attended conferences/presentations on women's issues.
    ( ) Have joined clubs or associations concerned with women's issues time available.
    ( ) Have not attended any of the above.

75. How would you rate your knowledge of the women's movement and women's rights in general?
    ( ) Very knowledgeable. (Please answer A)
    ( ) Somewhat knowledgeable. (Please answer A)
    ( ) Not very knowledgeable. (Skip to question 76)
    ( ) Not knowledgeable at all. (Skip to question 76)

A. Indicate the importance of the following sources of your awareness of women's issues by checking the appropriate column:

	very important	somewhat important	not very important	not important at all
• Newspapers and journals	_____	_____	_____	_____
• T.V. programs	_____	_____	_____	_____
• General courses in my field	_____	_____	_____	_____
• Courses dealing specifically with women's issues	_____	_____	_____	_____
• Presentations and informal conversations within the university	_____	_____	_____	_____
• Participation in feminist and professional organizations on campus	_____	_____	_____	_____
• Other (please specify)				
_____	_____	_____	_____	_____

76. Imagine yourself in the future, 15 years from now. How active are you likely to be in *both* the political and professional life of your country?

	very active	somewhat active	not very active	not active at all
In the political life	_____	_____	_____	_____
In the professional life	_____	_____	_____	_____

77. Still in the future 15 years from now, in what circumstances would you like to find yourself?
Check only *one*:
( ) Single, working full time
( ) Married, without children, not working
( ) Married, without children, working part time
( ) Married, without children, and working full time
( ) Married, with children, working part time
( ) Married with children, working full time
( ) Married, with children, not working
( ) Other (please specify)_____

78. Which of the following statements *best* describes the occupational condition of women in your country?
( ) Men and women are treated as equals in the job market
( ) The majority of women attain lower-status jobs than men
( ) Almost all women have lower-status jobs than men

79. Which of the following statements *best* describes the educational conditions in your country?
( ) Men and women attain the same years of education only at the primary level.
( ) Men and women attain the same years of education at primary and secondary levels.
( ) Men and women attain the same years of education at all levels (including university).
( ) There are inequalities between men and women at all levels of education.

80. How would you describe the educational experience of boys and girls in your country? (check one)
( ) The same is expected in education of girls and boys
( ) Teachers expect less of girls in science and math
( ) Overall, less is expected of girls
( ) Other (please explain)_____

THE STATEMENTS LISTED BELOW DESCRIBE A VARIETY OF ATTITUDES TOWARD THE ROLES OF WOMEN IN SOCIETY. THERE ARE NOT RIGHT OR WRONG ANSWERS, ONLY OPINIONS. PLEASE EXPRESS YOUR OPINIONS ABOUT EACH STATEMENT BY INDICATING WHETHER YOU AGREE STRONGLY, AGREE MILDLY, DISAGREE MILDLY, OR DISAGREE STRONGLY WITH EACH ONE

	agree strongly	agree mildly	disagree mildly	disagree strongly
Because of past discrimination against women in many kinds of jobs, they should be given preference over equally-qualified men.	_____	_____	_____	_____
A woman should be as free as a man to propose marriage.	_____	_____	_____	_____
A woman should not expect to go to exactly the same places or have quite the same freedom of action as a man.	_____	_____	_____	_____
In general, the father should have greater authority than the mother in bringing up the children.	_____	_____	_____	_____
A married woman should not accept a job that requires her to be away from home overnight.	_____	_____	_____	_____
Certain jobs should be done by women and certain jobs should be done by men.	_____	_____	_____	_____
Wife and husband should share the economic responsibility of supporting a family.	_____	_____	_____	_____
Women with small and school-age children should not work outside the home unless absolutely necessary.	_____	_____	_____	_____

WE HAVE NOW COME TO THE END OF THIS QUESTIONNAIRE. THANK YOU VERY MUCH FOR SHARING YOUR EXPERIENCES AND OPINIONS WITH US!

Appendix B

Questionnaire for Undergraduate Students

PLEASE NOTE THAT THIS QUESTIONNAIRE IS PRINTED ON BOTH SIDES OF THE PAGE. LET US BEGIN:

1. What is your country of origin?_____

2. Place where born: rural area_____   urban area_____

3. Age (check one): 18-22__   23-27__   28-32__   33-above__

4. Sex: ( ) Female   ( ) Male

5. You are now: ( ) a junior   ( ) a senior?

6. Degree in which you are currently enrolled:
   ( ) B.A.
   ( ) B.S.

7. Major(s) (specify)_____

8. Minor(s) (specify)_____

9. When did you declare your current major?
   ( ) Freshman year
   ( ) Sophomore year
   ( ) Junior year

10. How firm is your choice of field of study?
    ( ) Very firm
    ( ) Moderately firm
    ( ) Not very firm
    ( ) Will probably change

11. When did you develop an interest in your current field of study?
    ( ) Before coming to this country
    ( ) After coming to this country

12. How did you learn about your current field?
    _____
    _____

13. Why did you select your field? Check all the reasons that apply.
    ( ) Field will lead to definite employment opportunities.
    ( ) It is a field that will not create conflict with future family responsi-
        bilities.
    ( ) It is a field whose content interests me very much regardless of
        occupational potential.
    ( ) The admission criteria for this field are not very stringent.
    ( ) My family expects me to enter this field.
    ( ) Other (please specify)_____

14. Before coming to college, were you interested in pursuing another
    field of study?
    ( ) Yes
    ( ) No
    If yes, why did you not select it?_____
    _____

15. What is the *highest* level of education you expect to achieve?
    ( ) Bachelor's degree
    ( ) Master's degree
    ( ) Doctorate

16. Probable field and specialization if further studies are desired (please
    specify):
    _____

17. Why did you want to study in the United States?
    _____
    _____

18. How much encouragement did your parents give you for studying in
    this country?

	a great deal	some	a little bit	none at all
Father	_____	_____	_____	_____
Mother	_____	_____	_____	_____

19. Is your field of study available in the universities of your country? (check one)
   ( ) Yes (Answer A)
   ( ) No
   ( ) I don't know

20. How would you describe your field of study as it exists in your country?
   ( ) A field that traditionally attracts mostly women.
   ( ) A field that traditionally attracts mostly men.
   ( ) It attracts men and women in similar proportions.
   ( ) I don't know.

21. Are there women in professions related to your field of study in your country?
   ( ) Many
   ( ) Some
   ( ) Only a few
   ( ) None
   ( ) I don't know

22. Was the decision to pursue your current field of study mostly yours or was it influenced mostly by others?
   ( ) Most my decision
   ( ) Mostly by others

23. How important was each of the following persons in influencing your choice of field of study? (check the appropriate column for each)

	very important	somewhat important	not very important	not important at all
• Father	_____	_____	_____	_____
• Mother	_____	_____	_____	_____
• Teacher(s)	_____	_____	_____	_____
• School counselor	_____	_____	_____	_____
• Professionals in the field	_____	_____	_____	_____
• College peers	_____	_____	_____	_____
• Relatives/siblings	_____	_____	_____	_____
• Mass media	_____	_____	_____	_____
• Other (please specify):	_____	_____	_____	_____

24. Did anybody try to discourage you?
   ( ) No
   ( ) Yes   If yes, who? (please specify)_____

25. What reasons were given?
   _____
   _____

26. Prior to your choice of field of study, what kinds of activities did you engage in to prepare yourself for that choice? Check *as many* as apply.
( ) Talked to teachers about personal preferences and job opportunities.
( ) Talked to career counselor about personal preferences and job opportunities.
( ) Read books about professions and careers.
( ) Talked with professionals in my chosen field.
( ) No preparation took place.
( ) Other_____

27. Can you identify a particular experience as secondary student that significantly influenced your choice of field?
_____
_____
_____

28. What do you like *best* about the field you are in? Rank the three *most* attractive features, with "1" as the most attractive.
( ) The discipline is of great interest to me.
( ) The discipline requires math/science skills.
( ) The discipline requires verbal skills/English.
( ) The field offers many possibilities for finding a job.
( ) The field has high prestige.
( ) I like its competitive atmosphere.
( ) The field is not dominated by one sex.

29. What do you like *least* about your field? Rank the three *least* attractive features, with "1 as the most unattractive
( ) The coursework is very difficult.
( ) The field offers few possibilities for finding a job.
( ) The field requires math/science skills.
( ) The field requires verbal skills/English.
( ) The field has low prestige.
( ) I dislike its competitive atmosphere.
( ) The field is dominated by one sex.
( ) There is nothing I dislike about my field.

30. Is there anyone in your field whom you know personally and whom you consider an example to follow?
( ) Yes
( ) No

31. If yes, is this person ( ) a woman   or   ( ) a man?

32. Is this person from your country?
    ( ) Yes
    ( ) No

33. Why do you consider this person an example to follow?
    _____
    _____

34. Did you know this person before making your choice of field of study?
    ( ) Yes
    ( ) No

35. In your view, what is the **most** important feature of the occupation you plan to have?
    ( ) good salary
    ( ) chance to help others
    ( ) chance to be my own boss
    ( ) steady employment
    ( ) interesting work
    ( ) advancement possibilities

36. Do you anticipate obstacles as you seek to enter an occupation in your field?
    ( ) Yes
    ( ) No

37. If yes, what kinds of obstacles might emerge? Please elaborate.
    _____
    _____

NOW WE HAVE SOME QUESTIONS ABOUT YOUR EXPERIENCE AT THIS UNIVERSITY.

University where currently enrolled_____

38. How long have you been at this university?
    _____years_____months

39. Have you studied elsewhere in the United States?
    ( ) No
    ( ) Yes
    If yes, how many years?_____months_____
    Where?_____

40. Who pays for *most* of your education?
    ( ) Family   ( ) U.S. government
    ( ) This university   ( ) Myself
    ( ) Home government   ( ) Other_____

129

41. How would you describe your friendships with peers of your *own sex* at this university? Check the column that best describes these friendships:

	strong	moderate	weak	no friendship
In the area of social events	_____	_____	_____	_____
In the area of classwork/ studies	_____	_____	_____	_____

42. How would you describe your friendships with peers of the *other sex* at this university? Check the column that best describes these friendships:

	strong	moderate	weak	no friendship
In the area of social events	_____	_____	_____	_____
In the area of classwork/ studies	_____	_____	_____	_____

43. How would you describe your contacts with *faculty members* in your department?
   ( ) Very close
   ( ) Somewhat close
   ( ) Not very close
   ( ) No contact outside of class
       Why is this so?_____

44. How would you describe your contacts with *teaching assistants* in your department?
   ( ) Very close
   ( ) Somewhat close
   ( ) Not very close
   ( ) No contact outside of class

45. In your department, have you taken or are you taking courses taught by female professors?
   ( ) Yes
   ( ) No

46. In your department, have you taken or are you taking courses in which female students serve as teaching assistants?
   ( ) Yes
   ( ) No

47. How difficult is it for you to approach the following people? Check the column that best describes your degree of difficulty:

	very difficult	somewhat difficult	not very difficult	not difficult at all
Male professors	_____	_____	_____	_____
Female professors	_____	_____	_____	_____

48. How much support/advice regarding your current studies do you regularly get from the following persons? Check the column that best describes the amount of support/advise you get from each.

	very much	some	little	very little	I don't request it
Professors	___	___	___	___	___
Academic program advisor	___	___	___	___	___
Foreign student advisor	___	___	___	___	___
Fellow American students	___	___	___	___	___
Fellow international students	___	___	___	___	___
Non-university friends	___	___	___	___	___

49. If you have had problems regarding your *studies*, how would you rate the advice/support received from the following people?

	very effective	somewhat effective	not very effective	ineffective	I haven't requested help
Academic program counselor	___	___	___	___	___
Foreign student advisor	___	___	___	___	___
Professors	___	___	___	___	___
Fellow American students	___	___	___	___	___
Fellow international students	___	___	___	___	___

50. If you have had *personal problems* while attending this university, how would you rate the advice/support received from the following people?

	effective	somewhat effective	not very effective	ineffective	help not requested
Professors	___	___	___	___	___
Academic program counselor	___	___	___	___	___
Foreign student advisor	___	___	___	___	___
Fellow students	___	___	___	___	___
Non-university friends	___	___	___	___	___

51. Rate the degree of difficulty you have experienced at this university in the following matters. For each, check the column that best describes the degree of difficulty:

	very much difficulty	some difficulty	not very much difficulty	no difficulty at all
Financial issues: tuition remission, scholarships, loans, etc.	___	___	___	___
Fluency/ mastery of the English language	___	___	___	___

	very much difficulty	some difficulty	not very much difficulty	no difficulty at all
Mastery of math subjects	_____	_____	_____	_____
Faculty prejudices about the capabilities of Third World students	_____	_____	_____	_____
Racism on the part of faculty	_____	_____	_____	_____
Racism on the part of students	_____	_____	_____	_____
Sexual stereotypes on the part of the faculty	_____	_____	_____	_____
Other (please specify)				
_____	_____	_____	_____	_____

52. Generally, how have you solved these problems, if any?_____

_____

53. Can you suggest any ways in which your university could improve its performance to help you to succeed in your field of study? Be as specific as possible.

_____

_____

54. How many brothers do you have?_____brothers

55. How many sisters do you have?_____sisters

56. If you have older brothers and sisters who are studying in college or who already have a profession, please give their first name, field of study, sex, and age.

Name	Field of study	Sex	Age
_____	_____	__	__
_____	_____	__	__
_____	_____	__	__
_____	_____	__	__

57. Indicate your parent's *highest* level of education, by checking the appropriate column. (Answer this even if parent is dead.)

	incomplete primary	complete primary	incomplete secondary	complete secondary	Polytechnical/ incomplete higher edu.	B.A./ B.S.	M.A./ M.S. LL.B.	Ph.D M.D.
Mother's level of education	——	——	——	——	——	——	——	——
Father's level of education	——	——	——	——	——	——	——	——

Father's principal occupation/field_____

Title of father's position at work_____

Mother's principal occupation/field_____

Title of mother's position at work_____

58. If your mother does not now hold a paying job, has she ever worked outside the home? (including managing her own business or working in family business) (check one)
( ) Yes, she worked previously but not now
( ) No, she has never worked outside the home

59. If she has worked outside the home, what different jobs has she held? (describe as precisely as you can)
1 _____
2 _____

60. Please indicate how many *years* of the following you took in secondary school:
_____ math (including algebra, geometry and trigonometry)   _____ physics
_____ biology   _____ chemistry
_____ calculus

61. While in secondary school, your teachers were (check one):
( ) Mostly men
( ) Mostly women
( ) Equally men and women

62. Did you ever attend coeducational schools (serving both female and male students)? Please check all the statements that apply:
( ) I was never in coeducational school
( ) I was in coeducational school part of primary
( ) I was in coeducational school all of primary
( ) I was in coeducational school part of secondary
( ) I was in coeducational school all of secondary

63. How would you rate yourself relative to your peers back in *secondary* school in *math* ability?
    ( ) highest 1% of the class
    ( ) highest 10% of the class
    ( ) above average
    ( ) average
    ( ) below average

64. How would you rate yourself to your peers back in *secondary* school in *science* ability?
    ( ) highest 1% of the class
    ( ) highest 10% of the class
    ( ) above average
    ( ) average
    ( ) below average

65. If you worked for a wage or salary before coming to the university, what types of jobs have you held? (Please specify. If no job for pay, circle "3")
    1 _____
    2 _____
    3 Did not work for pay before coming to university.

66. If you have worked before as a volunteer (a non-paid job), what types of jobs have you held? (Please specify. If no volunteer jobs, circle "3")
    1 _____
    2 _____
    3 Did not work as a volunteer before coming to university.

PLEASE HELP US UNDERSTAND HOW YOU VIEW MARRIAGE AND CAREER OPTIONS. ANSWER ALL THE QUESTIONS BELOW, EVEN IF YOU ARE A MALE STUDENT.

67. If your future spouse were opposed to your working after marriage, what would you do? Check *one* statement.
    ( ) Choose marriage and forget career.
    ( ) Choose marriage and hope that spouse will change mind after marriage.
    ( ) Choose marriage and try to change future spouse's mind before marriage.
    ( ) Choose career and forget about marriage.

134

68. Do you expect the location and time requirements of your future occupation to conflict with family responsibilities?
( ) No, there will be no conflict.
( ) There will be a conflict, but my family needs will take precedence over career needs.
( ) There will be a conflict, but my career needs will take precedence over family needs.

69. At this university, which of the following activities have you undertaken? Choose *as many as* apply:
( ) Attended courses dealing with women's issues
( ) Attended conferences/presentations on women's issues
( ) Joined clubs or associations concerned with women's issues time available
( ) Have not attended any of the above

70. How would you rate your knowledge of the women's movement and women's rights in general?
( ) Very knowledgeable (Please answer A)
( ) Somewhat knowledgeable (Please answer A)
( ) Not very knowledgeable (Skip to question 71)
( ) Not knowledgeable at all (Skip to question 71)

A. Indicate the importance of the following sources to your awareness of women's issues by checking the appropriate column:

	very important	somewhat important	not very important	not important at all
• Newspapers and journals	_____	_____	_____	_____
• T.V. programs	_____	_____	_____	_____
• General courses in my field	_____	_____	_____	_____
• Courses dealing specifically with women's issues	_____	_____	_____	_____
• Presentations and informal conversations within the university	_____	_____	_____	_____
• Participation in feminist and professional organizations on campus	_____	_____	_____	_____
• Other (please specify)				
_____	_____	_____	_____	_____

71. Imagine yourself in the future, 15 years from now. How active are you likely to be in *both* the political and professional life of your country?

	very active	somewhat active	not very active	not active at all
In the political life	_____	_____	_____	_____
In the professional life	_____	_____	_____	_____

72. Still in the future and 15 years from now, in what circumstances would you like to find yourself?
    Check only *one*:
    ( ) Single, working full time
    ( ) Married, without children, not working
    ( ) Married, without children, working part time
    ( ) Married, without children, working full time
    ( ) Married, with children, working part time
    ( ) Married with children, working full time
    ( ) Married, with children, not working
    ( ) Other (please specify)_____

73. Which of the following statements *best* describes the occupational condition of women in your country?
    ( ) Men and women are treated as equals in the job market
    ( ) The majority of women attain lower-status jobs than men
    ( ) Almost all women have lower-status jobs than men

74. Which of the following statements *best* describes the educational conditions in your country?
    ( ) Men and women attain the same years of education only at the primary level.
    ( ) Men and women attain the same years of education at primary and secondary levels.
    ( ) Men and women attain the same years of education at all levels (including university).
    ( ) There are inequalities between men and women at all levels of education.

75. How would you describe the educational experience of boys and girls in your country? (check one)
    ( ) Teachers expect the same of girls and boys in all subjects.
    ( ) Teachers expect less of girls in science and math.
    ( ) Teachers expect less of girls in all subjects.
    ( ) Others (please explain)_____

THE STATEMENTS LISTED BELOW DESCRIBE A VARIETY OF ATTITUDES TOWARD THE ROLES OF WOMEN IN SOCIETY. THERE ARE NO RIGHT OR WRONG ANSWERS, ONLY OPINIONS. PLEASE EXPRESS YOUR OPINIONS ABOUT EACH STATEMENT BY INDICATING WHETHER YOU AGREE STRONGLY, AGREE MILDLY, DISAGREE MILDLY, OR DISAGREE STRONGLY.

	agree strongly	agree mildly	disagree mildly	disagree strongly
Because of past discrimination against women in many kinds of jobs, they should be given preference over equally-qualified men.	_____	_____	_____	_____
A woman should be as free as a man to propose marriage.	_____	_____	_____	_____
A woman should not expect to go to exactly the same places or to have quite the same freedom of action as a man.	_____	_____	_____	_____
In general, the father should have greater authority than the mother in bringing up the children.	_____	_____	_____	_____
A married woman should not accept a job that requires her to be away from home overnight.	_____	_____	_____	_____
Certain jobs should be done by women and certain jobs should be done by men.	_____	_____	_____	_____
Wife and husband should share the economic responsibility of supporting a family.	_____	_____	_____	_____
Women with small and school-age children should not work outside the home unless absolutely necessary.	_____	_____	_____	_____

WE HAVE NOW COME TO THE END OF THIS QUESTIONNAIRE. THANK YOU VERY MUCH FOR SHARING YOUR EXPERIENCES AND OPINIONS WITH US!

Appendix C

List of Fields of Study and Rating of Conventionality

**MAJOR CATEGORIES OF STUDY BY
FIELD AND SPECIALIZATION**

Field	Specialization	Conventionality Scale
A. MANAGERIAL		1
01 Accounting	01 Financial Accounting	1
02 Business Administration	01 Organizational Beh.	4
	02 Fin/Accounting	4
	03 Marketing	1
	04 Advertising	1
03 Business Communication	01 Mgt. Inform. System	3
04 Decision Systems		3
05 Finance and Business Economics		4
06 International Business	01 Intern. Finance	4
07 Food Industry Management		2

138

08	Marketing, Packaging			1
09	Advertising			1
10	Management and Organization			2
11	Library and Information Management	01	Academic Library	1
12	Organizational Behavior			2
13	Communication Management			2
14	Safety and Systems Management			4
15	Public Administration	01	Health Care Policies	1
16	Public Affairs	01	Economic Devel.	1
17	Labor and Industrial Relations			2
18	Operation Research	01	Statistics	2
19	Management Science	01	Applied Statistics	3
20	Social Science			0
21	Production Operation Management			2
22	Office Management			1
23	Hotel Management			1

B. TECHNOLOGICAL CAREERS — 3

01	Aerospace Eng.	01	Dynamics & Control	3
02	Surveying Eng.			4
03	Applied Mechanics			3
04	Biomedical Eng.	01	Laser Applicat.	3
05	Chemical Eng.	01	Process	3
		02	Electrochemistry	3
		03	Corrosion	3
06	Civil Eng.	01	Transportation	4
		02	Structure	4
		03	Geotechnical	4
		04	Building Scien. or Hydraulics	4
07	Computer Eng.			3
08	Computer & Informat. Sciences	01	Systems Programing	3
		02	Theoretical Comp.	3
		03	Language Theory	3
		04	Artificial Intell.	3
		05	Mathematical	3
		06	Theory & Computat.	3
		07	Graphics Animation	3
		08	Data Base	3
		09	VLSI Synthesis (Integrated circuits)	3
		10	Software Eng.	3
		11	Networks	3
09	Electrical Eng.	01	Communication	3
		02	Optic. Fiber Laser	3
		03	Microelectronics	3

		Code	Subcategory	
		04	Biomedical Instrum.	3
		05	Computer Eng.	3
		06	Robotics	3
		07	Artificial Intelli.	3
		08	Vision Image Processing	3
		09	Telecommunications	3
		10	Semiconductors	3
		11	Power	3
		12	Photonics	3
		13	Plasmas	3
		14	Microwave	3
		15	Electromagnetics	3
		16	Math Systems	3
		17	Signal Processing	3
		18	Control Systems	3
		19	VLSI	3
10	Environmental Eng.	01	Sanitation	4
11	Industrial/Systems Eng.	01	Manufacturing	3
		02	Health Systems	3
		03	Production	3
		04	Finance	3
		05	Ergonomics	3
12	Material Science Eng.			3
13	Management Eng.			3
14	Mechanical Eng.	01	Biomechanics	3
		02	Control	3
		03	Combustion	3
		04	Heat Transfer	3
		05	Design	3
		06	Solar Energy	3
		07	Agricultural	3
15	Mineral/Mining Eng.	01	Corrosion	4
		02	Soil Minerology	4
16	Nuclear Eng.	01	Design	4
17	Ocean Marine Eng.			4
18	Petroleum Eng.	01	Reservoir Eng.	4
19	Programing & Data Processing			3
20	Ceramics Eng.			3

C. EXACT SCIENCES

				3
01	Astronomy	01	Dynamic Control	3
02	Astrophysics	01	MM Radio	3
03	Chemistry	01	Organic	2
		02	Biochemistry	2
		03	Physical Chemistry	2
		04	Organic Synthesis	2
		05	Electrochemistry	2
		06	Inorganic	2

		02	Bacteriology	2
16	Animal Sciences	01	Animal Psychology	2
17	Botany			1
18	Medicine	01	Pediatrician	2
19	Pathology	01	Immunology	2
		02	Cell Biology	2

F. SOCIAL AND BEHAVIORAL SCIENCES

01	Anthropology			1
02	Communication Sciences & Disorders	01	Audiology	0
		02	Speech Pathology	0
03	Economics	01	Agricultural Economics	3
		02	Trade & Development	2
		03	Market Structure	2
		04	International Eco. & Finance	3
		05	Public Finance	2
		06	Macro Economics	2
		07	Labor Economics	2
		08	Consumer Economics	2
		09	Development Economics	3
		10	Econ. of Dev. Countries	3
		11	Applied Economics	3
04	East Asian Studies	01	Comparative Philosophy	1
05	Education	01	Administration	2
		02	Education	0
		03	ESL	0
		04	Child Development	0
		05	Counseling	0
		06	Curriculum & Instruction	0
		07	Computer-Based Training	2
		08	Educational Psychology	1
		09	Gender Studies	1
		10	Higher Education	1
		11	Home Economics	0
		12	Instructional Technology	1
		13	International Education	1
		14	Literacy	0
		15	Policy Studies	1
		16	Sociology of Education	0
		17	Statistics	1
		18	Teacher in Sciences	1
		19	Teacher in Agriculture	1
		20	Teacher in Math	1
		21	Special Ed.	0

		22 Physical Ed.	0
		23 Music	0
		24 Secondary Education	0
06	International Relat.	01 Middle East	3
		02 Latin America	3
		03 International Development	3
07	Middle Eastern Studies		1
08	Latin American Studies	01 Governt. Int. Business	2
		02 Economics	2
09	Political Sciences	01 International Relations	3
		02 Comparative Politics	3
10	Psychology	01 Personality/Clinical	1
		02 Educational Psychology	1
		03 Cognition, Memory & Perception	2
		04 Personnel/Organ. Psych.	2
		05 Social Psychology	1
		06 Measurement & Research	2
		07 Behavioral Neuroscience	2
		08 Intercultural Comm.	1
		09 Devl. Psychology	1
11	Sociology	01 Education	0
		02 Methods	1
		03 Rural	1
		04 Economy	1
		05 Conflict and Change	1
		06 Population Studies/ Demography	1
		07 Organizational Behavior	1
		08 Ethnic Relations	1
		09 Human Ecology	1
12	Social Work	01 Health	0
		02 Community Development	0
13	Social Policy	01 Comparative	2
14	Urban & Regional Planning	01 Transportation	2
		02 Housing	2
		03 Resources	2
		04 City Planning	2
15	African Studies		1
16	Political Sciences		3
G.	**HOME ECONOMICS**		0
01	Home Economics	01 Hospitality & Tourism	0
		02 Consumer Economics	0

		03	Family Resource Manag.	0
		04	Housing	0
		05	Human Nature	0

H. HUMANITIES — 0

01	History	01	Southeast Asia	0
		02	U.S.	0
		03	Asia	0
02	Languages	01	French	0
		02	African Languages	0
		03	Oriental Languages	0
		04	English	0
		05	Japanese	0
03	Linguistics	01	Syntax	0
		02	Sociolinguistics	0
		03	Tibeto-Burman Studies	1
		04	Computational Linguistics	1
		05	African Lang.	1
04	Literature	01	Black American	0
		02	Criticism	0
		03	Chinese	0
		04	Comparative	0
		05	Drama	0
		06	English	0
		07	Feminism	1
		08	Latin American	0
		09	Spanish	0
		10	Third World	0
		11	Spanish American Lit.	0
05	Philosophy	01	Medieval Philosophy	1
06	Religion/Theology			1

I. FINE AND APPLIED ARTS — 0

01	Art	01	Art History	0
		02	Graphic Arts	0
02	Fashion Design	01	Textile & Clothing	0
03	Interior Design/Applied Design			0
04	Music	01	Piano	0
		02	Composition	0
		03	Performance	0
05	Drama			0
06	Dance			0

J. COMMUNICATIONS — 1

01	Film, Cinema and TV Production	01	Intern. Comm. Culture	2
02	Journalism	01	Public Relations	0
		02	Agricultural Journalism	1

145

IIE RESEARCH SERIES

Report 1
ABSENCE OF DECISION:
Foreign Students in American Colleges and Universities
Craufurd D. Goodwin
Michael Nacht
(ED 232 492)

Report 2
BLACK EDUCATION IN SOUTH AFRICA:
The Current Situation
David Smock

Report 3
A SURVEY OF POLICY CHANGES:
Foreign Students in Public Institutions of Higher Education
Elinor G. Barber
(ED 240 913)

Report 4
THE ITT INTERNATIONAL FELLOWSHIP PROGRAM:
An Assessment After Ten Years
Marianthi Zikopoulos
Elinor G. Barber
(ED 245 635)

Report 5
FONDNESS AND FRUSTRATION:
The Impact of American Higher Education on Foreign Students
with Special Reference to the Case of Brazil
Craufurd D. Goodwin
Michael Nacht
(ED 246 710)

Report 6
INTERNATIONAL EXPERTISE IN AMERICAN BUSINESS:
How to Learn to Play with the Kids
on the Street
Stephen J. Kobrin
(ED 262 675)

Report 7
FOREIGN STUDENT FLOWS:
Their Significance for American
Higher Education
Elinor G. Barber, Editor
(ED 262 676)

Report 8
A SURVEY OF POLICY CHANGES:
Foreign Students in Public Institutions of Higher Education 1983-1985
William McCann, Jr.
(ED 272 045)

Report 9
DECLINE AND RENEWAL:
Causes and Cures of Decay Among Foreign-Trained Intellectuals
and Professionals in the Third World
Craufurd D. Goodwin
Michael Nacht
(ED 272 048)

Report 10
CHOOSING SCHOOLS FROM AFAR:
The Selection of Colleges and Universities in the United States
by Foreign Students
Marianthi Zikopoulos
Elinor G. Barber
(ED 272 082)

148

Report 11
THE ECONOMICS OF FOREIGN STUDENTS
Stephen P. Dresch
(ED 311 835)

Report 12
THE FOREIGN STUDENT FACTOR:
Their Impact on American Higher Education
Lewis C. Solmon
Betty J. Young
(ED 311 836)

Report 13
**INTERNATIONAL EXCHANGE
OFF-CAMPUS:**
Foreign Students and Local Communities
Mark Baldassare
Cheryl Katz
(ED 311 837)

Report 14
MENTORS AND SUPERVISORS:
Doctoral Advising of Foreign and U.S. Graduate Students
Nathalie Friedman
(ED 295 541)

Report 15
BOON OR BANE:
Foreign Graduate Students in U.S. Engineering Programs
Elinor G. Barber
Robert P. Morgan
(ED 295 542)

Report 16
U.S. STUDENTS ABROAD:
Statistics on Study Abroad 1985/86
Marianthi Zikopoulos
(ED 295 559)

Report 17
FOREIGN STUDENTS IN A REGIONAL ECONOMY:
A Method of Analysis and an Application
James R. Gale

Report 18
OBLIGATION OR OPPORTUNITY:
Foreign Student Policy in Six Major Receiving Countries
Alice Chandler

Report 19
SPONSORSHIP AND LEVERAGE:
Sources of Support and Field of Study Decisions
of Students from Developing Countries
Alan P. Wagner, Elinor G. Barber, Joanne King, and Douglas M. Windham

Report 20
PROFITING FROM EDUCATION:
Japan-United States International Educational
Ventures in the 1980s
Gail S. Chambers
William K. Cummings
(ED 320 488)

Report 21
CHOOSING FUTURES:
U.S. and Foreign Student Views
of Graduate
Engineering Education
Elinor G. Barber, Robert P. Morgan, William P. Darby
(ED 325 026)